Here Is What Church Leaders Nationwide Are Saying About

THE CHURCH OF IRRESISTIBLE INFLUENCE

"Finally, we get a clear picture of what the church of the twenty-first century should look like."

—Thom S. Rainer, *dean, The Southern Baptist Theological Seminary;*
president, The Rainer Group Church Consulting

"With winsome humility and hope, Robert Lewis proposes that our churches become bridges, and he offers an inspiring story of what that new orientation looks like and how it can happen in our churches today."

—Brian McLaren, *pastor, Cedar Ridge Community Church; author,*
The Church on the Other Side *and* Finding Faith

"Here is evidence that a church can be more than an island of righteousness in a sea of paganism."

—Dr. Erwin W. Lutzer, *senior pastor, The Moody Church*

"*The Church of Irresistible Influence* shows how a church can dare to bridge the gulf between good intentions and actual ministry. This will work with any church, anywhere, anytime, with people who learn to never say no to God."

—Jay Dennis, *pastor, First Baptist Church at the Mall, Lakeland, Florida;*
president, Florida Baptist Convention; author, The Prayer Experiment

"Robert Lewis paints an irresistible portrait of an influential church—and not from his imagination, but from a real working model."

—Tim Downs, *author,* Finding Common Ground

"Local church leaders will be very grateful for this coaching clinic on building bridges of irresistible influence to impact our culture."

—Dr. Stu Weber, *author,* Tender Warrior

"Don't think Robert Lewis is writing about some hypothetical and high-minded theory. It is quite a spiritual encouragement to personally experience the impact of such a church in the community and state where I live and work. Robert is a personal friend who has been both a 'Barnabas' and a 'Nathan' to me, and what he writes about in this book is exactly what he and his church have done. The ministry of Fellowship Bible Church touches me deeply and profoundly."

—Mike Huckabee, *Governor of Arkansas*

BRIDGE-BUILDING
STORIES
TO HELP REACH
YOUR COMMUNITY

THE CHURCH OF IRRESISTIBLE INFLUENCE

FOREWORD BY BOB BUFORD
ROBERT LEWIS WITH ROB WILKINS

ZONDERVAN™

GRAND RAPIDS, MICHIGAN 49530 USA

ZONDERVAN™

The Church of Irresistible Influence
Copyright © 2001 by Robert Lewis

Requests for information should be addressed to:
Zondervan, *Grand Rapids, Michigan 49530*

Library of Congress Cataloging-in-Publication Data
Lewis, Robert, 1949 Nov. 24–
    The church of irresistible influence / Robert Lewis with Rob Wilkins.
      p. cm.
    Includes bibliographical references.
    ISBN 0-310-25015-3 (softcover)
    1. Church work—United States.   I. Wilkins, Rob.   II. Title.
BV4403 .L49 2001
261'.1—dc21   00-068672

Published in association with the literary agency of Alive Communications, Inc., 7680 Goddard Street, Suite 200, Colorado Springs, CO 80920.

Interior design by Melissa Elenbaas

Printed in the United States of America

03 04 05 06 07 /❖ DC/ 10 9 8 7 6 5 4

To Bill Smith . . .

Life-giving encourager, supporter, cheerleader, and friend.

You, Bill, are the epitome of irresistible influence,

and for me, a treasured gift from God.

CONTENTS

ACKNOWLEDGMENTS

Most every book is a team effort, and this one is certainly no exception. Therefore, a special thanks is in order to those whose hard work has helped me produce this manuscript:

Kathy Helmers—Working with you, Kathy, was an absolute delight—and fun, too! Your support, encouragement, and professional counsel have been superb. But what I most enjoyed was our new friendship.

Rob Wilkins—We had a good year together, didn't we, Rob? Trips to Little Rock, cheering the Razorbacks, long talks about faith. I'm glad this turned out to be more than a writing project together.

Tracy Noble—No one cheers for me better than you do, Tracy! And no one can whip out a manuscript faster or better. Thanks for your willingness to fly up from Dallas to finish the job.

Nancy Carter—Few people encourage me as much as you do, Nancy. You are not only a talented artist, but a true servant of the church.

Dave Boehi—As always, I am deeply grateful for your excellent last-minute assistance.

The Board of Fellowship Associates—Thank you for your commitment to the churches of today and the church leaders of tomorrow. Steve Snider, you are an awesome leader! Ed and Judy, I believe your support will bear fruit for generations to come.

The ShareFest team—Rick Caldwell, Mona Thompson, Gary Jones, Paul Stevens, Ray Williams—you all "walk the walk." Thanks for bringing the churches of central Arkansas together.

The Nehemiah Group—Prayer summits. ShareFest. Hard work. Glory to God!

The People of Fellowship Bible Church—Could any pastor have a better body of believers? I don't think so.

I would also like to acknowledge five very special pastors who have uniquely influenced my life and shaped my thinking, while giving me the privilege of serving alongside them:

H. D. McCarty—University Baptist Church, Fayetteville, Arkansas, 1971–72

Bill Womersley—Christ Community Church, Tucson, Arizona, 1977–80

Bill Wellons—Fellowship Bible Church, Little Rock, Arkansas, 1980–2001

Bill Parkinson—Fellowship Bible Church, Little Rock, Arkansas, 1980–2001

Dan Jarrell—Grace Community Church, Anchorage, Alaska, 1994–2000

FOREWORD

The book you are about to read, *The Church of Irresistible Influence,* combines the stories of many of my own passions. They are passions that are directing my own ministry. They are passions that tug at many hearts that desire to see Christ lifted up.

First, I have a passion for strong congregations to be more effective. Through our work at Leadership Network, we have met with hundreds of leaders from large, highly effective congregations throughout the United States and Canada. For many years, we have followed the story of Fellowship Bible Church of Little Rock, Arkansas. Each year the story grows deeper and richer. I have enjoyed the vision, passion, and friendship of Robert and the other leaders there. Fellowship Bible is one of the great churches in America and one that all churches can learn from.

Second, I have a passion for people in Halftime. I wrote a book a few years ago by that title. The phrase describes individuals who realize they have lived their life chasing success but have not yet found the fulfillment they are seeking. They then begin a journey toward true significance. I have now heard from hundreds of business leaders around the world who have made the transition, through Halftime, from success to significance. We have been able to help some through our organization, FaithWorks. This book describes how dozens of members of Fellowship Bible

Church have made a similar journey. Their stories and examples are inspirational for all of us. I have been saying for some time that we are moving to an age where church life has shifted from proclamation to demonstration. The stories of the individuals in this book take the great preaching and teaching from their pastors and move it to real demonstration of Christ's love.

Third, I have a passion to see cities transformed. For the past few years, I have been following numerous city transformation efforts around the country. My observation is simply that when church leaders develop a heart for their cities, everything changes in how they view their calling and mission. They develop a kingdom mindset more than a church mindset. It calls them to deploy their resources (time, energy, people, dollars) into what I call a 50/50 church. This is a church where over half its resources are directed outward rather than inward. Many reluctant leaders feel this shift will eventuate in the weakening of the local congregation. Wise leaders know that the opposite is true. Following Christ's call to mission leads to strength. Fellowship Bible Church again leads the way in this movement. You will read how Fellowship Bible Church is taking the lead and working with other churches to transform their corner of the world.

Finally, I have a passion for this leader. Most of you will never get to spend time with Robert Lewis. Most of you will never get to observe his leadership up close. You will not get to see who he is in private. I have seen these things. The message and the messenger are true. Every time I speak with Robert, I am inspired about what he is doing and how he is leading his church. He will inspire you as you read this book. Take the ideas and try them in your corner of the world. It will make a difference.

BOB BUFORD
DALLAS, TEXAS

BEFORE YOU READ THIS BOOK ...READ THIS!

Imagination is a wonderful asset. It allows us to see realities as they "could be" and "should be." It relentlessly challenges us to go beyond our experience of what is, to those higher realms of the improbable. Robert Kennedy's words still stir me: "Some men see things as they are and say 'why?'... I dream of things that are not, and say 'why not?'"

No doubt you picked up this book because you have a love and concern for the church—perhaps as a pastor or board member, perhaps as a lay leader or interested layperson. The church of Jesus Christ is very important to you. It is to me too! So let me ask you to *use your imagination* for a few moments as you ponder the following questions:

- *Can you imagine* the community in which you live being genuinely thankful for your church?
- *Can you imagine* city leaders valuing your church's friendship and participation in the community—even asking for it?
- *Can you imagine* the neighborhoods around your church talking behind your back about "how good it is" to have your church in the area because of the tangible witness you've offered them of God's love?
- *Can you imagine* a large number of your church members actively engaged in, and passionate about, community service, using

their gifts and abilities in ways and at levels they never thought possible?

- *Can you imagine* the community actually changing (Proverbs 11:11) because of the impact of your church's involvement?
- *Can you imagine* many in your city, formerly cynical and hostile toward Christianity, actually praising God for your church and the positive contributions your members have made in Jesus' name?
- *Can you imagine* the spiritual harvest that would naturally follow if all this were true?

These are the visions, the "why nots" that constantly stir within my imagination. Some, I know, would call these dreams "impossible." I prefer to call them by another name—**"irresistible influence"**—i2 for short. And i2 is not a dream; *it's real!* i2 is a symbol drawn from Jesus' words in Matthew 5:16 that has powerfully captured the imagination of the people of Fellowship Bible Church and turned our faces and our attention outward to good works. The results have been transforming, revolutionary, and often surprising. We are not only reconnecting with the people and needs of our community as "salt and light" (Matthew 5:13–14), but we are also reconnecting with a long-neglected part of our Christianity: the part that believes that the Great Commandment to "love your neighbor as yourself" (Matthew 22:39) is just as essential to the spread of the gospel and to the sanctification of church members as the Great Commission (Matthew 28:18–20).

i2 (**irresistible influence**) is about the great need that exists today of reconnecting the church with the community in a way that makes the church both *real* and *reachable*. I believe the church can only accomplish this by turning outward and loving those around us the way Jesus loved his world: not just in words, but with deeds. Scripture says that against such love, "there is no law" (Galatians 5:23). Love is irresistible—irresistible influence.

By 1990 anyone observing our growing church would probably have characterized it as a great success. In little more than ten years, Fellowship Bible Church had grown from a mere handful of people to over 2,500. "Successful" was a word frequently used by both outsiders and insiders when describing our congregation.

But even with all our advances over ten years, we were still little more than a stranger to our community. Honestly, the larger we had become, the more preoccupied we had become—with ourselves. It would be hard to imagine that this was the design Jesus had in mind when he dreamed of his church. And as a pastor, I increasingly felt the uncomfortable dissonance of this loss. I longed for our church to have more of the cultural impact that one experiences from the pages of the New Testament and at particular points in history. But how?

The Church of Irresistible Influence describes this journey. It has been a trial-and-error, sometimes painful, sometimes chaotic experience that has constantly demanded from us both faith and courage.

But, with i² as our vision, we have also experienced something else—something holy. It has radically altered our church's perspective from "in" to "out." And the transformations that have followed are significant and worth telling.

Let me offer some advice here that will help you navigate your way around this book. First, you will quickly notice that each chapter is introduced by a "bridge story." Frankly, I cannot think of a better metaphor for what the church of Jesus Christ is biblically designed to be than that of a bridge. You will also discover in reading these stories that successful bridge building and successful church building have some remarkable similarities. You could say these bridge stories are my own modern-day *church parables.* They are arranged to illustrate for you the central truth of each chapter. So enjoy them. But also let them drive home the fact that today's church must once again become to every community a carefully crafted bridge if it expects to connect with real influence.

Second, you will note throughout each chapter that I have set apart key statements for you to ponder. These statements can also take you through a chapter quickly in summary form or remind you of its highlights.

Third, I have provided "Bridge Builder Questions" at the end of each chapter (except for chapters 7 and 8) to help you apply what you have learned to your own particular church setting. If this book is studied by your church board or church leadership team, these "Bridge Builder Questions" can serve as helpful discussion starters.

Finally, as you can see in the table of contents, I have broken this book into five parts:

- **Part 1:** "Spanning the Great Divide" documents the increasing disconnect today's church—especially the evangelical church—is experiencing with modern culture. This section will also offer what I believe is the simple but profound solution to this crisis of distance: proof.

- **Part 2:** "Designing the Structure" will be of great interest to those who want to know *how*—in practical terms and applications—a church can reinvent itself and move its people into the community with influence.

- **Part 3:** "Experiencing the Results" consists of real-life stories drawn from the last five years of i² in action. Those of you who love stories might want to sample one or two of these narratives in chapter 6, 7, or 8 before starting at the beginning.

- **Part 4:** "Expanding the i² Effort" will explain how our i² journey has led us into some surprising new partnerships, particularly with other churches. If you want to catch a glimpse of how unity among churches can powerfully reach and influence a whole city in a way that feels thoroughly like the New Testament, start by reading chapter 9. I think you will be greatly encouraged.

- **Part 5:** "Anticipating the Future" describes the strategic moves I believe the church must make in the twenty-first century if it is going to be a cultural leader rather than a follower. For some of you who may be concerned that this book already sounds too much like the "social gospel," I strongly suggest that you start by reading chapter 12. I believe it will answer your concerns theologically, while providing a balanced perspective that you can take with you in reading the rest of the manuscript. Still, let me say straight up: I do not believe in a social gospel that seeks to save the world through human compassion and good works. My trust is in Jesus Christ *alone*.

But I also believe in that wonderful theological reality called *sanctification*. I believe it is impossible to be personally sanctified without "love and good deeds" (Hebrews 10:24). Moreover, "faith without deeds is dead" (James 2:14–26). And any proclamation to the world of the love of God without authentic incarnation is hollow. We need both. And both is what irresistible influence— i² —is about.

I love the church of Jesus Christ. I love the truth it stands for. I love the life it alone can give. Despite its shortcomings due to the open arms it offers sinners, it still remains the greatest force on earth for good. Nothing else is like it or can match it, *especially* when it is healthy. It alone possesses the supernatural message of truth that can transform the worst of humanity in an instant, while unleashing the best of it over a lifetime.

But today's church is losing its grip on the very world it has been called to save. Why? Why are we experiencing this growing disconnect?

This is where we must begin. . . .

PART ONE

SPANNING THE GREAT DIVIDE

What Will It Take

to Reconnect

the Church

and Culture?

CHAPTER 1

THE GREAT CHASM

The church's inward focus is a grave illness.

—**Michael B. Regele**, *Death of the Church*

A BRIDGE STORY

In 1851 many of the most accomplished engineers in the country thought James Roebling was out of his mind. That year Roebling began to work on the unthinkable: the bridging of the Niagara River Gorge.

Disaster was nearly universally predicted. There was, of course, the sheer mathematics of the thing: 825 feet across, and—more terrifyingly—200 feet down. Straight down. As in a plummet you couldn't even dream in your worst nightmare.

But the numbers paled in comparison to the sheer power and raging terror of the place. Roebling's proposed site was just upstream from the great Niagara Falls, where up to 37.4 million gallons of water per minute fell into the Niagara Gorge. From there the rushing water had cut a deep abyss with a series of savage rapids before ending in a tremendous whirlpool held in a massive rock basin. A no-man's-land.

Across such a chasm, Roebling believed a train could cross.

History was not a powerful ally. Although greater spans had already been bridged—including Roebling's own bridge across the Ohio River—the Niagara River posed fierce difficulties: No girders or bridge supports, provided that they could even be constructed, would ever survive the raging current. The only possible solution, to Roebling, was a suspension bridge.

And that was what had people worried. At the time, suspension bridges were about as well regarded in the engineering profession as the Edsel would be in the early automotive industry—disasters in the making. They shook in the wind, and after a few years they twisted and crumbled into the waters they were designed to span. In England and France suspension bridges had collapsed under the mere weight of crossing humans, killing hundreds. In America a number of small suspension bridges—mostly for the movement of livestock—had collapsed, including one over the Licking River in Covington, Kentucky.

When Roebling first proposed a suspension bridge across the great Niagara Gorge, it came as no great surprise that most people were putting their money on the gorge, not the bridge.

The Chasm was simply too great, too terrible.

As THE CHURCH ENGAGES a third millennium, it too looks across a terrifying—and ever-widening—chasm:

- Between first-century authority and postmodern skepticism;
- Between a bold proclamation of God's love and unmet human needs;
- Between the selfless vision of Christ and the self-obsessed reality of our world;
- Between the truth of God's laws and the moral compromise of our culture;
- Between those who believe and those who don't.

At the bottom of the chasm rages the white water of popular sentiment, which increasingly views the church as inconsequential, a sideshow along the interstate of the world's *real* traffic. Today, "numerous studies confirm that the public, especially media and intellectual leaders, do not see Christianity as a dominant social force."[1] Instead, six out of ten Americans believe the church is irrelevant.[2] And in the lives of the 170 million non-Christians in America (making our country the third largest mission field in the world), that irrelevance provokes an ever-increasing cynicism and hostility.

A growing sense of isolation and powerlessness pervades much of the contemporary church. Have you felt that as a pastor or layperson? A sinking feeling that we are not only losing ground but losing our voice as well? If so, you're not alone. As it stares across the Great Chasm, much of the church no longer believes it can greatly influence the world.

In fact, only one out of three pastors—*pastors*—believes the church is making a positive impact on the culture.[3]

RESORTING TO FALLBACKS

Often, as "engineers of churches," pastors and lay leaders desperately desire to bridge the gap, but when measuring the gorge with the world's mathematics, they come to believe the span is simply too vast. I personally have often felt paralyzed by the intimidating distance that exists between the church and the community here in Little Rock. The sheer size of the Great Chasm is not only intimidating, but it also scares many church leaders into believing that the task is impossible. As a result, many pastors resort to the following "fallback methodologies" as substitutes for spanning the great divide:

As it stares across the Great Chasm, much of the church no longer believes it can influence the world.

"Be Culturally Relevant." According to this strategy, churches can best address their receding influence through contemporary repackaging. Unfortunately, this strategy often goes too far. It becomes relevance at the expense of substance. In many contemporary churches, believers no longer carry Bibles. Worshipers seek an experience with God minus the commitment. Therapy replaces morality. Entertainment crowds out the cross. Is it maturity we're after, or the "feel good"? "These new paradigm churches," David Wells says, "appear to be succeeding not because they are offering an alternative to modern culture, but because they are speaking with its voice and mimicking its moves."[4]

"Promise Heaven Now." Pastors and traveling speakers tell eager audiences that God promises health, wealth, and power to anyone with enough faith. Churches with this strategy certainly draw a crowd. And why not? Who wouldn't want this? But is this the Christian life or the American Dream in pseudospiritual garb?

"Just Preach the Word." I love expository preaching and deeply admire those who do it well. But great preaching *alone* will not reach our world or magically transport unbelievers across the Great Chasm. According to Rick Warren, there are many who say, "If you'll just stay doctrinally pure, preach the Word, pray more, and be dedicated, then your church will explode with growth. It sounds so simple and so spiritual, but it just isn't true."[5]

To make matters worse, those in the world often see believers who are "under the Word" falling woefully short of the supernatural lifestyles the Scripture presents. In a recent poll, George Barna, a sociologist and research expert, compared the lifestyles of Christians and non-Christians, using 131 different measures of attitudes, behaviors, values, and beliefs. His conclusion: "In the aspects of lifestyle where Christians can have their greatest impact on the lives of non-Christians, there are no visible differences between the two segments."[6]

How will the world ever discover church again if what they see across the Great Chasm is, in reality, people no different than themselves, living in what appears to be a fantasy? "Our gospel," laments Dr. Henry Blackaby, author of *Experiencing God,* "is cancelled by the way we live."[7]

"Stay the Course." Believing that the world influences the church too much and often discounting the obvious, many decide to stick with the same "tried-and-true" methods that they've used for decades. One pastor friend of mine stated this methodology succinctly when he said, "If the 1950s ever come around again, my church will be ready." What is sadly overlooked is that these older methodologies were originally created to work only in a certain time and context. Some were no doubt considered radical departures from the norm in their own day. But no longer. Yesterday's freshness always fades. What's worse, "doing business as usual" today is a complete denial of the crisis at hand. Charles Chaney, former vice-president of the Southern Baptist Home Mission Board, is right when he says, "America will not be won to Christ by establishing more churches like the vast majority we now have."[8]

I do not wish to be harsh. Some of what is happening in today's church has brought important and long overdue additions to the Christian agenda: culturally sensitive messages from the Word, helpful adaptations of technology, deeper development of community, a recovery of the arts, and a greater attention to real personal needs. Our own church has adopted parts of these strategies. But what we have failed to do, for the most part, is to bridge the Great Chasm.

The question was simple: What impact is the church having on the community?

For all its frenetic activity and supernatural posturings, the overall impact of the church on American culture is generally understood to be about the same: just slightly above zero. "I believe it is time to confess that our strategies have not worked," says Michael B. Regele, cofounder of Precept Group, Inc., an organization that has developed congregational profiles for nearly 20,000 churches. "Church leaders are working harder and harder for fewer positive results."[9]

Recently I conducted an informal poll at a suburban mall near where I live in Little Rock, Arkansas. The question was simple: What impact is the church having on the community? When I posed that question to a teenager, his answer was direct and penetrating: "The church," he said, "is crap." We want to indignantly react or piously defend ourselves, appealing to the few success stories we know. But across the Great Chasm, can we hear the truth in his voice?

A DANGEROUS DREAM

As James Roebling peered across the Niagara River Gorge, he believed the chasm could be bridged. Even with an abundance of naysayers, some of his confidence rested in this verifiable fact: it had already been done. Within a short distance of his proposed railroad bridge, a suspension bridge already hung, although a bit shakily. The work of Charles Ellet, American engineer and showman, the bridge had opened three years before Roebling strung his first cable. Ellet had proved, at the very least, that the Great Niagara Gorge was vulnerable.

A master of ingenuity and flamboyance, Ellet solved his first problem—how to get the initial wire across the gorge—with characteristic pomp and style. He offered the first American boy to fly a kite across the chasm a five-dollar reward. The competition was intense as skies over thundering waters were filled with frail colors, but on the first day, no one was successful. On the second day, young Homer Walsh won the prize. The string of his kite was fastened to a tree on the far side of the river, a light cord attached to it, and pulled slowly back over the gorge. Next came a heavier cord, then a rope, and finally a cable composed of number 10–strand wires. It was the beginning of Ellet's bridge, the accomplishment of a soaring dream.

Ellet was not finished with the dramatics. After the first cable was completed, he decided to demonstrate his faith in an unforgettable fashion. He built an iron basket, attaching it to the cable with a series of pulleys. Then he got inside, pulling himself across—the first man ever to cross the great chasm. "The wind was high and the weather cold," he wrote of the experience, "but yet the trip was a very interesting one to me—perched up as I was two hundred and forty feet above the Rapids, and viewing from the center of the river one of the sublimest prospects which nature had prepared on this globe of ours."[10]

Along both rims of the gorge on that historic March day, an excitement surged through crowds. They had witnessed the accomplishment of the impossible.

Still Ellet was not finished. After a catwalk had been completed several weeks later, he leaped into a small horse-drawn carriage and rolled fearlessly headlong onto the tiny bridge with, as yet, no guardrails. Standing straight up like a charioteer, Ellet directed the carriage across the bridge, which swayed fearfully. In the crowds, women passed out, men stood dumbstruck, and, in the end, applause was heard over the gorge's roar.

As Roebling pondered his much larger bridge, Ellet's efforts must have generated some confidence. Yet it was to be a short-lived reassurance. In May 1854—just one year before the completion of Roebling's bridge over the Niagara Gorge—word was received that a suspension bridge over the Ohio River, also built by Ellet, had collapsed. It had survived just five years.

Jesus was a daring bridge builder of another kind. Against his own overwhelming odds, he imagined a bridge of unprecedented spiritual influence.

Most people were now convinced that James Roebling was a dangerous dreamer. Could it be doubted that the Great Chasm would win in the end?

Jesus Christ was a daring bridge builder of another kind. Against his own overwhelming odds, he imagined a bridge of unprecedented spiritual influence—one that could span a chasm roaring with skepticism, indifference, hostility, even persecution. He imagined a bridge able to connect his people—"my church," he called them—to a disbelieving, disinterested world.

That's why Jesus loved to talk about the church, especially the power it could unleash and exercise in the world.

Follow me, he would say, *and I will make you fishers of men.*

You are the light of the world, he would teach, *shine in the darkness.*

You are the salt of the earth, he declared, *make a tasteful difference.*

Nothing, he believed, would prevail against the power of the church: *I will build my church,* he said, *and the gates of hell will not overcome it.*

By exhibiting, through everyday humanity, his life and love to the world, Jesus expected the church to supernaturally attract all men to God: *If I am lifted up,* he said just before his death, *I will draw all men to myself.*

This is the bridge Jesus imagined: a connecting church—a bridge of influence.

EQUIPPED FOR WHAT?

The message of this book is simple: the church must rediscover its essential role and craft as bridge builder. For the world's sake. For the church's sake. For God's sake. We can no longer simply afford to stand on one side of the Great Chasm and shout to those on the other side. We must connect. Otherwise, the greatest unbridged chasm will remain the gap between the stunning vision of Jesus Christ and the ever-receding influence of the contemporary church in the world.

> *The church must rediscover its essential role and craft as bridge builder. . . . We must connect.*

As pastors and lay leaders, as engineers, we must recommit ourselves to dangerous dreaming and precise calculating. We must be a people of deep faith. *The great chasm can be bridged!*

To a very small degree, I know from personal—and often painful—experience. Our own church, Fellowship Bible Church in Little Rock, Arkansas, has built its bridges mostly by trial and error. We have suffered through numerous collapses. But we continue making the attempt. And with our own "dangerous dreams," progress is being made.

At first, however, we didn't even understand that bridge building was what we were *supposed* to be doing. Our church, from its start in 1977, implemented many ministry concepts that only recently have come into vogue in today's contemporary church models: team preaching; small groups; lay equipping and empowerment; passionate worship; strong, focused vision; seeker-sensitive evangelism; results-oriented planning—all with a deep commitment to biblical accuracy and truth.

The process of personal transformation, we firmly believed, only occurred within the boundaries of the supernatural Word of God and an ever-intensifying relationship with God in all of his triune glory, power, and excellence. We believed, too, that spiritual growth happened in the context of honest, loving relationships. We stressed that all of our people should be involved in small groups where other Christians could know them well enough to encourage them deeper into the life and love of God.

Church leaders also took seriously the duty to "equip the saints." We sought to meet needs, help people discern their gifts, build skills and confidence, increase knowledge, and develop spiritual and personal authenticity. And in fact, we still believe all of these issues are critical to the work of the church.

And yet, to be quite frank, an essential piece of the puzzle was missing. In 1989 the church reached a crisis point. With an intuitive sense that something was wrong, we as leaders of the church engaged in a formal study. Our people were surveyed through a multifaceted questionnaire. The results were stunning. We discovered that after four to five years of involvement in the small group ministry that is central to our church, people began to feel unchallenged and stifled. Their excitement about church dramatically declined. They had always been told that they were to be "equipped," but the data raised a greater question:

"Equipped *for what?*"

In the history of our church, nothing has shocked us as much as that simple, three-word question. It was like a bomb went off inside the church walls, one that would eventually lead to a complete reconstruction of Fellowship Bible Church.

FAULTY DESIGN

As our elders discussed the survey with our congregation and sought guidance from the Word of God, we realized we were at a crossroads.

If we continued on our present path, we would likely create a style of ministry that we would one day regret. We would eventually function as a refuge from the world, a sort of Christian "club" that exhausted itself trying to keep its members happy. We would become focused on our own inward needs. We would probably measure our success, not by the true biblical standards of courage and faithfulness, changed and changing hearts, and an irreplaceable impact on the world through good works, but rather by other things: personalities, numbers in attendance, entertainment value, money, and facilities. We would become the type of church described by Bill Hull in his book, *Can We Save the Evangelical Church?* "The average evangelical church in North America exists for itself," Hull writes. "Churches are preoccupied with themselves, their routines, facilities, and filling their buildings for performances."[11] Yes, we could certainly go there.

Or, we realized, we could make a bold, radical move in a new direction. We could courageously pursue the type of church Jesus envisioned.

We saw more clearly than ever before that our church members were unchallenged and stifled because they were cut off from their divine mandate of bridge building. It was easy to understand why so many evangelical Christians sound strange, while looking so much like everyone else. Trapped in the small and mirrored room of introspection, reduced to the size of his or her own appetite, the average Christian has precious little motivation for real, radical change. With the Great Chasm uncrossed, the focus inevitably shifts from the transformed and compelling life—the necessity of becoming salt and light in a needy and searching world—to a much more superficial desire to "look Christian" to other Christians.

In a sense, we felt we had been running a basketball camp. With all the difficult and sometimes tedious focus on training, skill development, conditioning, and position selection, we had never actually played the game. In all our activity and hard work, we had missed the bigger picture.

We were missing our highest calling: *to bridge the Great Chasm!* But that quickly changed. Soon church structure was being reorganized, new staff were hired, and people were asked to take their first intimidating steps outside the safe and comfortable environs of the church campus we had been so consumed in building. The answer to the question, Equipped for what? came down to the simplest of answers: "For God so loved *the world.*"

The church, we now firmly believe, is to be in the bridge-building business, according to the design of Jesus Christ. Over this bridge the church must travel and *prove* its reality to a disbelieving world. Only then will the world reconsider its skepticism, hostility, and lostness. Our world must experience the same incarnational influence as the first century experienced when Grace and Truth himself suddenly bridged that Great Chasm and became flesh.

Bridge building is much different work than success building.

But bridge building is much different work than success building. Let me say this with as much of the humility birthed from our own difficult experiences as I can: If the church functions with any other design than that of a bridge, it dooms itself. Our hard work over time will sink into the cold waters of irrelevancy, frustration, and despair. Great, charismatic preaching will drown in isolated, self-absorbed hearts. Innovation and cutting-edge technology without a new vision will become like a pile of rusted saltwater shipwreck. I am aware of how strong this sounds, but I believe it is only as judgmental as, say, a man who tells a child on a roof that his arms are not wings, or an engineer who rules out the circle for road design.

The necessity of understanding the church's design as a bridge is critical. Imagine a great city without its bridges—New York City with no crossing of the Hudson and East Rivers, or San Francisco minus the Golden Gate, or London without the London Bridge, or Paris without a way to traverse the Seine. *Bridges give life through two-way movement!* Without its own bridges to the world, church life—in time—fades into isolation, self-congratulation, and finally, irrelevance.

> *Without its own bridges to the world, church life—in time—fades into isolation, self-congratulation, and finally, irrelevance.*

KEEPING FAITH

James Roebling, in a sense, was a man of faith. He believed in the fixed laws of the universe. If great chasms refused to be bridged, it was the fault of the engineers, not the structures. Despite accumulating evidence to the contrary, Roebling insisted, "There are no safer bridges than those built on the suspension principle, if built understandingly, and none more dangerous if constructed with an imperfect knowledge of the principles of their equilibrium."[12]

Roebling's bridge was completed in March 1855. It was profound both in its simplicity and economy: "four plain towers sixty feet high [on opposing banks], four cables ten inches in diameter, their suspenders and stays, and a straightforward timber truss joining the two levels to the one span."[13] The bottom level was for carriage and pedestrian traffic, the top reserved for the Great Western Canada Railroad.

On Friday, March 16, the first train crossed over. Put together especially for this purpose, it was far heavier than most trains—the engine weighed twenty-eight tons, and it pushed twenty double-loaded cars. A few days later a passenger train, packed to capacity and beyond, also made the journey, this time from Canada to the United States.

Roebling harbored a quiet but deep satisfaction. He reveled in the opening of such great commerce, but even better, the separation that had long existed between two strong countries had been spanned. He was pleased with the harmony, economy, grace, and soundness of its structure. But most of all, he revisited its elemental purpose. "No one," he wrote to his family, "is afraid to cross."[14]

The impossible became possible. A keeper of his faith, Roebling was now believed.

Jesus said, "I tell you the truth, anyone who has faith in me will do what I have been doing. He will do even greater things than these, because I am going to the Father" (John 14:12).

As we turn to face the Great Chasm, can we believe him?

BRIDGE BUILDER QUESTIONS

What kind of impact do you believe today's church is having on our culture?

How does the community around you "know" your church? Do they feel a positive connection with it?

What tangible influence is your church having on your community?

CHAPTER 2

LIVING PROOF

Faith is an island in the setting sun

But proof, yes

Proof is the bottom line for everyone

—**Paul Simon**

A BRIDGE STORY

For the job of bridging the Mississippi River, the résumé of James Buchanan Eads did not naturally surface:

Engineering degree: none.
Bridges built: none.
Work experience: underwater salvage, a glass factory (which was closed down), gadabout, gunboat builder, and river boatman.

Yet shortly after the Civil War, when the City Council of St. Louis declared it "indispensably necessary to erect a bridge across the Mississippi River," Eads was chosen for the job. More renowned and distinguished candidates, such as Charles Ellet and James Roebling, who had both constructed suspension bridges across the Niagara River Gorge, were turned down.

Slim, leathery, given to strong opinions, often disliked, Eads had at least two things going for him:

unbridled self-confidence, and an unmatched knowledge of the river itself. Wrote one writer, "He managed to convince men who had worked with the country's foremost engineers that he, James B. Eads, was the one man fit to bridge the Mississippi at St. Louis [and] that the bridge that he wanted to build was the only answer."[1]

The city was gambling its entire future on a novice. At the time five railroads from the east and three from the west converged on St. Louis. The only way for the trains to cross was via barge, one railroad car at a time. By bridging the Mississippi, St. Louis would be a national artery and would secure a lifeblood of new commerce.

Roebling, for one, was dumbfounded by the city's risk. Considered to be perhaps the country's greatest engineer, Roebling had not just one but two sets of plans turned down. Miffed and confused by the city's choice of Eads, Roebling would later write to his son that "St. Louis people were fools."[2]

The bridge proposal of Eads, like the man, was indeed radical, unorthodox, and untested.

- *Instead of suspension or iron truss design, which was customary for railroad bridges at the time, Eads proposed an arched bridge that would cross the river in just three mammoth spans, the largest of which would exceed a record distance by more than 100 feet.*
- *The arches, resting on massive stone piers, would gain their needed strength from two untested ideas—at least in terms of bridge building—one old, the other new: the cantilever ("canted-lever") principle (originally articulated by Galileo in the seventeenth century), and the use of steel.*
- *He would build the bridge with little disruption to boatmen, for whom he had great empathy.*

And for all of that, said his critics, he might just as well sprout wings from his back and fly across the river.

One consultant to Eads, Jacob H. Linville, the bridge engineer for the Pennsylvania Railroad and an undisputed authority, did not believe Eads's ideas would work. He wrote, "I cannot consent to imperil my reputation by appearing to encourage or approve of its adoption." He added that he deemed such a bridge as "entirely unsafe and impracticable."[3]

After beginning construction, the running joke in neighboring saloons soon became "the bridge that would take seven million dollars to build—and seven million years."

But Eads had a history of prevailing. He had gone from poverty to wealth to poverty and back to wealth. He could play chess with three men at once and win each game. In a weight-lifting contest with blacksmiths, the wiry Eads placed second, with plans for a rematch. But he wasn't counting on his brilliance or power to build the bridge. He possessed a far greater power: a knowledge of the Great River itself, which, since his birth, he had been in, around, under, and over. At deep and shallow levels, he understood the river. And with the wisdom of the river in his mind and body, he knew—like no one else could—what it would take to bridge it.

In response to his critics, Eads coolly responded, "Must we admit that because a thing never has been done, it never can be, when our knowledge and judgment assure us that it is entirely practicable?"[4]

Proof, he knew, would come.

IN OUR POSTMODERN AGE, the chasm between the church and world is best gauged by a flow of consciousness, not distance. The chasm itself is not a benign void but a raging river of thought called relativism. Nothing is certain; anything goes.

It didn't used to be so. Even less than a century ago, the church—banked against a kinder, gentler river—could more easily bridge the gap between itself and the world. It had the public's trust and admiration, which allowed it to speak with authority. The church, in fact, was often at the center of community life and comfortably ahead of all spiritual rivals. Even if it did not convert every unbeliever, the church exercised a formidable influence on morals and on understanding the distance between right and wrong. Whatever the issue, the church most often connected with the community on the well-established bridge of absolute truth.

But no longer. The foundational pillars of truth have eroded away. Pilate, perhaps the first postmodernist, was a man truly ahead of his time. When you attempt to communicate absolute truth in today's culture, you will get his kind of bewildered response—stitched eyebrows, a tilt of the head, a flash of anger or perplexity: *"Truth. What is truth?"* It is the same sense of incredulity an American might get speaking Spanish in Paris.

I have learned this lesson about truth the hard way. For half of my pastoral ministry, I believed my mission was to help the world understand its errors. Like so many other similarly afflicted evangelicals, I thought by hurling verbal hand grenades concerning sin and wrongdoing into the world, the shrapnel would somehow rattle sinners back to their senses. To me, jabbing and stabbing the world with the sword of what I considered impeccable logic and reasoning, backed by God's Word and a dash of holy anger, was the way to turn the world around.

To me, jabbing and stabbing the world with the sword of . . . God's Word and a dash of holy anger was the way to turn the world around.

In those days I never built much of a bridge into the world. Like many churches, we advertised—impersonally inviting the uninitiated to courageously "seek us out." The community also felt our occasional "hot breath" concerning issues like abortion, pornography, and other specific social ills—a disembodied voice of judgment.

But after years of doing so, it began to dawn on me that my actions—no matter how sincere—were not merely ineffective, but they were, in fact, fueling an even greater hostility and alienation between our church and the community. I was *burning* bridges, not *building* them.

As I analyzed the problem, I realized that my first error was in *trying to convince a postmodern world of truth when it rejects truth,* especially when it is presented from a distance. In our culture, nothing is regarded as completely right or completely wrong. Increasingly, truth is consistently and wrongly defined as a matter of one's preference or perspective, if it exists at all.

But this shouldn't surprise us. This worldview has been brewing for hundreds of years. Absolute truth began to pass away at the time of the Renaissance and the Reformation, explosive transitions that shattered Western civilization's presupposition of a singular worldview based principally on biblical revelation as presented by Roman Catholicism.

At those significant moments, competitive views of absolute truth arose—some religious, some secular. For centuries, fierce debates raged—sometimes involving brutal wars, sometimes political edict or law—to determine winners and losers. By the dawn of the twentieth century, the modern age arrived in full, and the church found itself in a titanic struggle for truth with an increasingly popular and pragmatic rationalism.

With some logic, the church believed it must argue for truth if it hoped to continue building bridges with secure foundations. So for most of this century, the evangelical church in particular worked hard at defending the faith—which the Bible defines as "the evidence of things not seen"—against a soulless rationalism that, through the cold calculation of science, dismisses whatever cannot be derived through the senses.

In the end, no one won.

Rationalism lost out because of the very science on which it depended. Today we witness new scientific discoveries continually undermining "the facts" of previous ones. It becomes more and more clear: no assumption is safe. As one writer put it, "The era of dogmatic scientific certainty is gone."[5] Therefore, nothing in rationalism is ever "for sure." Tomorrow's research is the constant enemy of today's bold certainty. It has led, in the words of George Weigel, to the "unsecularization of the world," which he describes as "one of the dominant social facts in the late twentieth century."[6]

The church also lost. Many of its basic claims, of course, are unsupportable without a leap of faith. So how is this different from any other religion? Its doctrines, some poorly presented and others less and less lived out, were increasingly seen as out of step with a modern age; its methodologies, old and tired. And to add injury to faith, many of its deeds were shown by the "objective" media to often be the work of hucksters, hypocrites, fanatics, or idiots.

Enter postmodernism. An age of utter skepticism—to everything! An age hostile to absolute claims from any source. An age of hard reality, not oversold proclamations. An age, in the words of singer Paul Simon, where "proof is the bottom line for everyone." An age where even reason—and maybe especially reason—has been drowned in the swirling and turbulent eddies of experience. *I think, therefore I am,* has been replaced with *I feel, therefore I know . . . maybe.*

> *This is the first time a civilization has existed that, to a significant extent, does not believe in objective right and wrong.*

In his book, *Losing Our Virtue,* David Wells observes, "This is the first time a civilization has existed that, to a significant extent, does not believe in objective right and wrong."[7]

THE POWER OF THE GREAT RIVER

Under the muddy and turbulent waters of the great Mississippi lay sunken treasure from ships that had sunk over the years. But few people tried to find it. The problem was the great and devouring hunger of the river itself. The constantly shifting sandy bottom, and the wild and unpredictable currents and undercurrents would quickly cover up a wreck, shifting it to just about anyone's guess. Treasure was elusive—difficult to find, let alone to salvage.

At the age of twenty-two, Eads had an idea. In his head, and then on paper, he developed a design for a diving bell. Although divers had been successfully using diving bells to explore the bottoms of calm lakes, the swift currents of the Mississippi made it impossible to maintain control. To solve the problem, Eads loaded a forty-gallon whiskey barrel with a few hundred pounds of lead. Across its open end, he fashioned a strap, allowing the diver to sit. Eads himself had to test his device; he could not find a diver willing to ride this mad-looking contraption. Using a submerged double-hulled snag boat as base and a diving bell with air pressure pumped into it, Eads eventually had a crude but effective means of walking the river's bottom and, more importantly, of salvaging lost cargo. In addition to making a fortune, Eads gained a wealth of wisdom about the river. Over the next few years, he made more than five hundred dives.

Eads's experiences resulted in one certain fact: more than any man alive, he intimately knew and understood the Mississippi. And with the wisdom of the river in his mind and body, he knew—like no one else could—what it would take to bridge it.

Our postmodern world is tired of words. It wants real. Real is everything. Real is convincing.

As an engineer of bridges between the church and the world, it is the responsibility of the church leader to understand—first and foremost—the spirit and forces of the age. As every great engineer knows, there is no such thing as a "standard" bridge; each is custom-made to a unique set of conditions in a specific area during a particular time. Each has to be postured and fitted to the terrain, weather conditions, distance, anticipated traffic, and—most important—purpose.

We as church leaders must understand the same principle: the very life of the church is intertwined with a recognition of the times. I am fearful that by clinging to what is cherished or what seems successful, many pastors and/or their church boards refuse to embrace what is vital. The loss is predictable, tragically comic, and overwhelming—the church ceases being an influence on society. Our salt becomes tasteless, our light hidden.

Church leaders everywhere sense this. At one large gathering of pastors in our area, the questions asked were: Are we really making a difference? Is our influence growing? Is the moral tenor of our community changing because of us? Not one man could muster a convincing "Yes."

Why?

Years ago, when I was evaluating my own effectiveness as a bridge builder, I realized that, in this postmodern culture, the church often lacks the credibility necessary for our age. We continue in our attempt to blindly build bridges to our world solely on a disembodied truth model.

But to our age, truth is nothing more than talk—especially when you don't show it. The eye, not the ear, is the decisive organ. Our postmodern world is tired of words—it wants *real*. Real is everything. Real is convincing.

And yet, real is something the church seems less and less geared to demonstrating, much less producing. What we *are* geared to is slicker, more technologically brilliant presentations of truth. But the *real* truth is, where is the love of God we talk about? Where is the transforming power of Christ? The changed lives? The selfless giving? The good works? While the world waits to *see* it in their communities, the church is consumed with *talking* about it in their sanctuaries.

This is why we are not spanning the chasm and connecting with the community. We are trying to build bridges on truth alone, while the world is crying out for proof. *Proof!*

Our design is wrong. We need bridges that balance public proclamation with congregational incarnation. Bridges that are suspended by the steel cables of the Great Commandment as well as the Great Commission. In the twenty-first century, the church must understand, as never before, that faith—without works—is dead. So, too, will be our influence.

> *In the twenty-first century, the church must understand, as never before, that faith—without works—is dead.*

As a result, the chasm between the church and the world only grows wider and more disingenuous. Says George Barna, "Americans are not going to patronize an institution which appears incapable of living what it preaches."[8]

I believe we need to accept the fact that the world has dramatically changed. We need to recognize, and not ignorantly fight against, what is inevitable. If we could finally accept change, we could begin to look at, and not ignore, the issue of postmodernism. And we would see, much to our surprise, that the chasm is not invulnerable. It can be bridged. We do not, as many think, live in an age that despises belief. Rather, it is an age that *wants to believe,* desperately so. Deeply disillusioned by the failure of human reason and logic, it is open to outside—and even supernatural—explanations. But it trusts nothing except what it can see and, more importantly, *experience.*

For the watching world, drowning in postmodernism, this is foundational: not simply the Word of truth, but the Word made flesh. A living proof—an irrefutable incarnation.

BUILDING THE CORRECT FOUNDATION

For bridge support, James Eads had two choices. He could work from above and build a suspension bridge, or from below and build down into the river. Neither option was promising; both had never before been accomplished on such a daunting scale.

While James Roebling had proved that a suspension bridge could handle railroad traffic, the span of the Mississippi was much greater than that of the Niagara. In fact, at 1,524 feet compared to 825 feet, it was nearly doubled. With existing technology, it seemed impossible.

But focusing down into the wild and unpredictable nature of the great Mississippi itself seemed equally daunting. Nevertheless, down Eads went. For his steel arches, based on a cantilever principle, to work, the great stone piers Eads constructed would have to face great stress not only from the raging river but from the bridge itself. Everything depended on the strength of the foundation. If the piers could not withstand the raging and continual currents, the bridge would eventually crumble and disappear. The proof of Eads's design would come only after an extended period of time.

I believe a fitting description for the church would be this: *a community of people who stand firm in the truth over time against raging currents of opposition and who present living proof of a loving God to a watching world.* While that may not describe many churches today, it could serve as a textbook definition for the church of the first century.

The New Testament church shared many cultural similarities with our own. It too lived in a world filled with skeptics. For a number of

> *I* believe a fitting description for the church would be this: a community of people who . . . present living proof of a loving God to a watching world.

41

reasons, the lifeless gods and goddesses of the Greeks and Romans became less and less a prevailing force in the lives of the ancients. As economic prosperity flourished, the souls of everyday men and women increasingly descended into a meaningless poverty.

Enter the gospel of Jesus Christ, the Word made flesh, the living proof of God. Enter Christians who embraced the Word and, like their Lord, lived it out in word *and* deed—proof positive to a once proud and now decaying culture that there was, in fact, a better, nobler life. Proclamation was more a matter of essence—in life and death—than it was an enunciation of words. Believers stood firm, often with great sacrifice, in good works anchored by the exhortations that now flow from the pages of the New Testament:

Let Everyone See Your Good Deeds

In the same way, let your light shine before men, that *they may see your good deeds* and praise your Father in heaven.

MATTHEW 5:16

Love Your Enemies, Do Good to Them

Do to others what you would have them do to you. If you love those who love you, what credit is that to you? Even sinners love those who love them. And if you do good to those who are good to you, what credit is that to you? Even "sinners" do that. And if you lend to those from whom you expect repayment, what credit is that to you? Even "sinners" lend to sinners, expecting to be repaid in full. But *love your enemies, do good to them,* and lend to them without expecting to get anything back. Then your reward will be great, and you will be sons of the Most High, *because he is kind to the ungrateful and wicked.*

LUKE 6:31–35

It Is More Blessed to Give

In everything I did, I showed you that by this kind of hard work we must help the weak, remembering the words the Lord Jesus himself said: *"It is more blessed to give than to receive."*

ACTS 20:35

Overcome Evil with Good

On the contrary: "If your enemy is hungry, feed him; if he is thirsty, give him something to drink. In doing this, you will heap burning coals on his head." Do not be overcome by evil, but *overcome evil with good.*

ROMANS 12:20–21

Do Good to All People

Let us not become weary in doing good, for at the proper time we will reap a harvest if we do not give up. Therefore, as we have opportunity, *let us do good to all people.*

GALATIANS 6:9–10

Created to Do Good Works

For we are God's workmanship, created in Christ Jesus to *do good works,* which God prepared in advance for us to do.

EPHESIANS 2:10

Do Not Grow Weary of Doing Good

But as for you, brethren, *do not grow weary of doing good.*

2 THESSALONIANS 3:13
(NASV)

Be Rich in Good Deeds

Command those who are rich in this present world not to be arrogant nor to put their hope in wealth, which is so uncertain, but to put their hope in God, who richly provides us with everything for our enjoyment. Command them *to do good, to be rich in good deeds, and to be generous and willing to share.* In this way they will lay up treasure for themselves as a firm foundation for the coming age, so that they may take hold of the life that is truly life.

1 TIMOTHY 6:17–19

Engage in Good Deeds

This is a trustworthy statement; and concerning these things I want you to speak confidently, so that those who have believed God may be careful to *engage in good deeds.*

TITUS 3:8 (NASV)

Be Eager to Do What Is Good

For the grace of God that brings salvation has appeared to all men. It teaches us to say "No" to ungodliness and worldly passions, and to live self-controlled, upright and godly lives in this present age, while we wait for the blessed hope—the glorious appearing of our great God and Savior, Jesus Christ, who gave himself for us to redeem us from all wickedness and to purify for himself a people that are his very own, *eager to do what is good.*

TITUS 2:11–14

Spur One Another to Love and Good Deeds

And let us consider how we may *spur one another on toward love and good deeds.*

HEBREWS 10:24

Be Eager to Do Good

Who is going to harm you if you are *eager to do good?*

1 PETER 3:13

BRIDGES OF PROOF

With lives intertwined with proclamation and incarnation, those first believers effectively penetrated the empty hedonism of the ancient world. And no matter how reactive the pagan world—first with skepticism, then with isolation, and finally with the sword of brutal persecution—these bridges of proof, anchored in good works, convinced more and more to walk over into eternal life. It is estimated the early church grew at an astounding 40 percent growth rate per decade.[9]

All historians of the early church link this compelling witness of proof to the explosion of early Christianity. Listen to Michael Green:

> The link between holy living and effective evangelism could hardly be made more effectively. In particular, Christians stood out for their chastity, their hatred of cruelty, their civil obedience, good citizenship. . . . They did not expose infants, they did not swear. They refused to have anything to do with idolatry and its by-products. *Such lives made a great impact.* Even the heathen opponents of Christianity admitted as much. . . . It is difficult to overestimate this moral emphasis in the growth of second century Christianity.[10]

Shaunti Feldhahn summarizes Princeton University sociologist Rodney Stark's similar observations from his book, *The Rise of Christianity.* Noting the extraordinary expansion of Christianity in the first and second centuries, "[Stark] was puzzled at how a marginalized, persecuted, often uneducated group of people were able not only to survive, but thrive. . . . He concludes that a key reason was their willingness to sacrifice themselves out of love for each other and for their world. This sacrifice released an explosion of light and heat the world had never known."[11]

All historians in the early church link this compelling witness of proof to the explosion of early Christianity.

Stark's article in *Christian History* shows the powerful proof Christians offered during the two great plagues that swept the Roman Empire in the years A.D. 165 and 251, killing a third of the population each time. He writes:

> The willingness of Christians to care for others was put on dramatic public display. . . . Pagans tried to avoid all contact with the afflicted, often casting the still-living into the gutters. Christians, on the other hand, nursed the sick, even though [some] died doing so. . . . Christians also were visible and valuable during the frequent natural and social disasters afflicting the Greco-Roman world: earthquakes, famines, floods, riots, civil wars, and invasions. Even in healthier times, the pagan

emperor, Julian, noted the followers of The Way "support not only their poor, *but ours* as well."[12]

Historian Will Durant makes this additional observation:

Never had the world seen such a dispensation of alms as was now organized by the Church. . . . She helped widows, orphans, the sick or infirm, prisoners, victims of natural catastrophes; and she frequently intervened to protect the lower orders from unusual exploitation or excessive taxation. In many cases, priests gave all their property to the poor . . . others devoted fortunes to charitable work. The church or her rich laymen founded public hospitals on a scale never known before. . . . *Pagans admired* the steadfastness of Christians in caring for the sick in cities stricken with famine or pestilence.[13]

High morals, superior lifestyles, good works, sacrificial acts of love. Against raging currents of opposition in the ancient world, the message of the gospel nevertheless exploded because it was built over a bridge of living proof.

Said Tertullian, an early church father, "Men proclaim that the state [Roman Empire] is beset with us. We are only of yesterday, but already we fill the world."[14]

A BRIDGE, SENSATIONAL AND TECTONIC

A well-designed and flawlessly constructed bridge is a collective work of art. With each part in harmony, performing a specific and complementing function, structure and flexibility in wonderful tension, and a precise economy of function and material, a bridge is a marvel to behold. Its building, in the spanning of a void, becomes a work of powerful influence.

Nowhere was this more true than in the bridging of the Mississippi in 1874. With much fanfare and fireworks, the bridge, anchored securely against the raging currents of the Great River, was officially opened on July 4. Praise was everywhere. Louis Sullivan, a famous architect, called it "sensational and tectonic."[15] Walt Whitman, the poet, extolled the "perfection and beauty unsurpassable" of its structure.[16]

Under a fifty-foot poster of Eads hanging from the bridge was an understated plaque that read: "The Mississippi, discovered by Marquette, 1673; spanned by Captain Eads, 1874."[17]

In my quest to discern how my pastoral ministry could be more effective, I saw that more preaching is not the answer to today's spiritual hunger. Neither is the writing of more books, the hosting of more conferences, better technology, or special effects. For the most part, we are simply talking to ourselves. Meanwhile, the church grows increasingly isolated from its community and the culture, glorying in a biblical "witness" it often does not really possess.

Then I looked at some of the early attempts by our church at serving and caring for our community.

- *I noticed* the changed lives that resulted from members investing their lives in helping families in a low-income area known as Eastgate.
- *I observed* the impact of doctors from our church who set up a medical clinic at a home for unwed mothers.
- *I felt* a sense of God's pleasure as I joined hundreds of our members as we went out into the community one Saturday to clean up neighborhoods, repair homes, and complete other projects.
- *I noted* that city leaders were beginning to view Fellowship Bible Church as a force for good in the community.
- And wonderfully, *I saw* people who were formerly hardened to, and skeptical of, the gospel soften and embrace Christ.

I realized that we didn't need to be slicker or trendier to draw people in our community to Christ, but better and holier. We didn't need to invest time and money into more events, but reinvest it into equipping our people to live genuinely good lives. We didn't need to be more religious; we needed to be more *connected.*

That was a turning point for me and for our church. From that point on, I told our congregation, I would "put much less time into pointing out the world's errors and much more time into proving God's love."

What the world waits to see is whether what we have is better than what they have.

Risky? Yes. But I confess, the world is tired of the church impersonally talking it down and chewing it up. What the world waits to see is whether what we have is better than what they have.

Just think what bridges we could build if we truly followed the example of the New Testament church. We would go beyond being seeker-sensitive, to a new frontier of being community-admired. We would be known, not just by the corner we inhabit, but by the city with which we interact. And people would be drawn to God, not because of the weekly show in our churches, but by the irrefutable lifestyles we incarnate.

On both sides of the postmodern chasm, there is a growing emptiness. For the church, it is due to a lack of radical, courageous, and sacrificial faith: *If our Christianity is real, let's live it.* For the world, this emptiness is from a lack of captivating, life-giving proof: *If your Christianity is real, let's see it.*

A bridge is needed. But not just any bridge. A bridge of proof. How to construct such a bridge is the topic we will explore in our next three chapters.

BRIDGE BUILDER QUESTIONS

What kinds of "living proof" has the community around you experienced of your church's Christianity?

How would the call of "living proof" in the community challenge the way your church presently operates?

Read again the Scriptures and historical quotes listed in this chapter. What helpful perspectives and ideas do they stir up in you?

PART TWO

DESIGNING THE STRUCTURE

The How-Tos of

Incarnational

Bridge Building

CHAPTER 3

JESUS AND THE IDEA OF IRRESISTIBLE INFLUENCE (i²)

> *There is one thing stronger than all the*
> *armies in the world; and that is,*
> *an idea whose time has come.*
>
> —Victor Hugo

A Bridge Story

In the 1850s, near the height of the gold rush, San Francisco, with its noble clipper ships, brawny steamers, and fluid ferries, was a picture of maritime prosperity. Enmeshed in prosperity and expansion, no one was contemplating the thought of building a bridge across the Golden Gate. Why? It would be impossible, for one thing, and completely unnecessary, for another. You would have to be crazy to think otherwise.

But that's exactly where the ideas for the Golden Gate Bridge originated.

In 1859 Joshua Norton, who had lost a fortune from gold and a good part of his mind in the process, became the first to suggest that such a bridge was needed. Norton was not just a bit of a nut, he was the real deal. As one author put it, "In San Francisco's legendary galaxy of eccentrics, he was the shining star."[1]

Once a respected businessman, he was driven mad by his misfortune. In 1859, after years of seclusion, he emerged with an announcement, printed in the San Francisco Bulletin, that "at the preemptory request and desire of a large majority of citizens of these United States" he claimed the office of Emperor. Later, perhaps bored with such a limited reign, he added "Protector of Mexico."

In mock submission, the city of San Francisco "gleefully submitted to his rule," affording him the privileges of royalty, including free meals and opening night theater tickets. He stood, dressed in military-style clothing, as nonsensical nobility. He was the King of Fools.

Of the many "proclamations" of Emperor Norton, his most famous was a call for a suspension bridge across the Golden Gate. This was his decree:

PROCLAMATION

WHEREAS, it is our pleasure to acquiesce in all areas of civilization and population: Now, therefore, we, Norton J. *Dei Gratia* Emperor of the United States and Protector of Mexico, do order and direct first, that Oakland shall be the coast termination of the Central Pacific Railroad; secondly, that a suspension bridge be constructed from the inprovements lately ordered by our royal decree at Oakland Point to Yerba Buena, from thence to the mountain range of Saucilleto and from thence to the Farallacones, to be of sufficient strength and size for a railroad; and thirdly, the Central Pacific Railroad Company are charged with the carrying out of this work, for purposes that will hereafter appear. Whereof fail not under pain of death.

Given under our hand
this 18th day of August, A.D. 1869.

Norton I. Emperor

Norton Emperor Theliest

Great ideas sometimes start off in a touch of madness. Remember: They even accused Jesus of being a little out of his mind.

MORE THAN BY DECADES or centuries, history is marked by great ideas; that is, when someone, placed in unique culture and circumstance, stands up and says, "What if we believed—and acted upon—*this?*" Luther's idea of grace. Gandhi's idea of nonviolent resistance. Ford's idea of efficiency. Hitler's idea of nationalism. Einstein's idea of relativity. Jesus' idea of the church.

Few men saw the power of an idea more clearly than Napoleon, a small man with big ideas. "Men do not rule," he said. "*Ideas* rule!"

An idea is more than a starting point; in a deep sense it is everything. An idea strong enough to spark imagination, inspire sacrifice, build faith, and encourage perseverance is the most powerful human force on the planet. It has the power to determine the future—for good and for bad.

Power unleashed can never exceed the power embedded in the idea. Power of idea, then, equals power of potential influence. This is true no matter what you are doing: building an empire, a philosophy, a bridge, or a church.

Let us consider the power of just one idea: Darwin's theory of evolution. It soon spawned an equally powerful idea that chance, not God, originally sparked life. Millions of years and a process known as natural selection have helped life evolve to what it is today. For a religious world in the mid-nineteenth century, this was a shocking, arrogant idea. But from that singular thought, the world was dramatically altered.

Ideas, for good or for bad, rule us!

The idea that man was a unique creation of an all-powerful God was suddenly overturned in the minds of many. Especially among intellectuals, this new idea of our origin was positively exhilarating. With it, man was no longer tethered to divine reward or retribution, or to an oppressive church, or to the fixed laws of Scripture. Man, finite as he might be, was free to pursue a utopia of his own making. And at the beginning of the twentieth century, that utopia seemed to be just within modern man's ever evolving reach.

This idea also laid the philosophical groundwork for a host of powerful social movements, the most dominant of which was communism, which promised its eager followers a man-made society of equality and justice void of God and religion. This too was an exhilarating idea, but with horrendous, awful consequences. And while most of the world has now discarded communism into the trash bin of history—after decades of war, human slaughter, ruthless tyranny, spiritual deprivation, and finally, dismal failure—we still live in a world dominated by Darwin's idea of life and the offspring it continues to propagate. It is certainly the bedrock foundation for the worldview of most of today's scientists, political theorists, and social engineers.

Napoleon was right. Ideas, for good or for bad, rule us!

Scripture makes the point this way: "As [a man] thinks within himself, so is he" (Proverbs 23:7). Our thoughts both drive us and define us. Our ideas, in time, become our realities.

JESUS' BIG IDEA

Our ideas also become our churches. How we see them in our mind's eye, to a large degree, determines their look, their feel, their success or failure.

The driving idea behind Fellowship Bible Church, which has developed and evolved over twenty-plus years, has now been compressed into two taps on a keyboard: i^2. The church, we believe, should be a force of *irresistible influence* in its community. By building bridges of real spiritual integrity between itself and an increasingly skeptical society, we possess the power and authority to be a catalyst for change and an engine of influence.

But with the church's credibility faltering and an increasing number of Christians living no differently than anyone else, this idea, at first, seems to be an oxymoron. A church of irresistible influence? You might just as well pair Hollywood with family values or the government with efficiency. In the world where we happen to live, it just doesn't happen.

Irresistible influence was Jesus' Big Idea.

So an i^2 church starts with a courageous question: Do you believe—and not just *say* you believe—what Jesus said about the church?

Irresistible influence was Jesus' *Big Idea*. He envisioned that the church would possess and exercise it. He illustrated it through multiplying loaves and fish (Mark 8:1–8). He commanded it by telling his disciples to fan out across the world and make disciples (Matthew

28:18–20). He promised it to Peter, "On this rock I will build my church, and the gates of hell shall not overcome it" (Matthew 16:18). I particularly love this promise because it shows the church in its rightful posture, on the offensive, battering the gates of evil that are holding a city, and breaking through.

Jesus preached influence. In his very first sermon, he made influence for his future church his central theme: "You are the salt of the earth.... You are the light of the world" (Matthew 5:13–14). We could easily paraphrase him to say, "You are to be an infectious influence!" Without it, he warned, you are "no longer good for anything, except to be thrown out and trampled by men" (Matthew 5:13).

Nowhere can we escape this idea of irresistible influence: the church as i².

ANOREXIC MODELS

I believe there's the sake of both!

Contrary to much evidence, the church does not exist for the sake of the church. It exists for the sake of the world. Unfortunately, many contemporary churches, unable to bridge this gap of relevance to the world, have either resigned themselves to irrelevance or, even more troubling, redesigned themselves after two other types of "big ideas."

The first "big idea" driving many churches is to create a church that meets the needs of its members. And since so many people have such deep spiritual needs, there is much good in this approach. But often it also leads to unhealthy consequences. Needs soon turn to wants. A toxic self-absorption can easily develop. "Us" becomes all that matters. Spiritual impact is rarely contemplated beyond the borders of the church property. Like a star that has collapsed into a black hole, refusing to release its light, a "need-meeting church" can unknowingly come to exist for nothing bigger than itself.

> *A "need-meeting church" can unknowingly come to exist for nothing bigger than itself.*

Is that stated openly? Absolutely not! Sermons instead often recount Christianity's glorious missionary advances, its courageous sacrifices, and its world-changing impact. But like young men reading great books instead of engaging real life, it speaks from memory, not experience. Michael Regele, a researcher, writes:

Leadership, within this current church model—and people hate me for saying this—basically functions as the board of directors of a social club. They are very serious and well intentioned, but they have created a social structure that exists solely to care for the Christians that are members of their church. Such questions as "What does evangelism mean?" and "What does discipleship mean?" . . . seem like luxuries in that kind of environment.[2]

Under the banner of this first idea, priorities are determined by internal needs, desires, and finally, wants. The most important things soon become an endless stream of self-serving events, activities, and facilities. Build the new Family Life Center. Church league softball. Concerts. Trips. Seminars. Camps. Food fairs. In a church club, members huddle closely together around a common campfire, but by doing so, they block the essential light. Martin Lloyd-Jones writes:

> The whole purpose of lighting a light is that it may give light. And for a foolish man to cover it with something which prevents that quality from manifesting itself is, we are all agreed, utterly ridiculous. Yes; but remember that our Lord is speaking about us. There is obviously a danger, or at least a temptation, that the Christian may behave in this completely ridiculous and futile manner, and that is why He emphasizes the matter in this way. He says, "I have made you something that is meant to be like a light. . . . Are you deliberately concealing it?" . . . To do this is to render ourselves completely useless.[3]

A second "big idea" driving many contemporary churches is the concept of success. Seeking conformity to a culture dominated by commerce, the "success" mentality is simple: the bigger, the better. Size matters. Numbers count. More is what is always needed: more people, more facilities, more staff, more money. It is a mostly polite game of Christian Darwinism: the survival of the fittest, or the church with the greatest attendance. The goal is to be in the elite class known as the "biggest church in the city" or "Top 10 in the denomination" or "megachurch." Such churches often spend increasing amounts of money and energy putting on elaborate events to draw more people in.

While correctly pointing out that churches, when healthy, should be dynamically growing, pride often infuses the "success" church with a twisted irony: the church might be recognized nationally, but it often remains *a stranger to its very own community.* Influence, which is often large, is exercised mostly within "the greater

> *A successful church often remains a stranger to its very own community.*

church." Of the successful church, few questions are asked. More people are coming. More money is being given. More staff is being added. More buildings are being built. More programs are starting. What could possibly be the problem?

Churches driven by either of these big ideas become, in truth, islands without bridges—spending their influence mostly on themselves in an isolated and disconnected world. Stuffed full, they reduce themselves to the margins of a culture, a footnote on a local Chamber of Commerce pamphlet. They have nothing to say and no way to say it in the very communities in which they are rooted. The best that can be mustered is the launching of empty words, like deflated balloons, untethered to the community: "Join us this Sunday" . . . "Jesus loves you" . . . "Come to _____ event." For those outside the church, these words float by like leaves in a winter wind.

LIFESTYLES OF THE SPIRITUAL AND AUTHENTIC

In the early days of Fellowship Bible Church, a driving big idea seemed elusive. Quite frankly, we knew more of what we *didn't* want than what we did. Besides, like most raw "start-ups," we were simply focused on survival. The only bridges we raised were the ramps we used to move equipment.

Without a facility of our own, wandering first from a small school and then to a movie theater, we had little time to think, much less envision. Besides maintaining sanity, the other deep commitment we shared was a desire for authentic, God-indwelt Christian lives. It was what, in fact, brought us all together as college students in the late 1960s at the University of Arkansas.

As one of those college students, I can testify that our fellowship was deep and passionate. In fact, for many of us this spiritual pursuit to know Christ together often took precedence over everything else, including our education. Upon graduation, we each struggled to find a church that could offer us a similar experience. We craved open, honest relationships. We desired the lofty ideals that we often read about in the Scripture for our personal lives, our marriages, our pursuits. We wanted to be real.

In our first few years out of college, we were stunned to find our church experiences both disappointing and lackluster. It was this disappointment and the hunger for something more that brought some of us back together in Little Rock in the summer of 1977. There, in the living room of Don and Sally Meredith, eighteen courageous people decided to launch Fellowship Bible Church with ideas borrowed from Gene Getz and his church, Fellowship Bible Church in Dallas.

In 1982, after several hard years of challenging start-up efforts, our young but growing congregation felt the need for some kind of "Big Idea" of our own, a mission statement that would offer both an identity and a sense of direction to our fledgling body. Here is what we originally settled on:

> We exist to manifest the reality of Christ to the world by equipping Christians to live lifestyles of spiritual integrity

As mission statements go, it was neither catchy nor slick. What it expressed was a sincere desire on our part to equip our people to pursue an authentic, biblical Christian lifestyle. Even then, in images half recognized, we were beginning the work of dreaming dangerous dreams. The way we live, we were saying, should build bridges of proof. Lifestyles of spiritual integrity—like the preservative nature of salt, and the revealing qualities of light—were, in our minds, the catalysts of certain influence. Had not Jesus guaranteed this?

Without practically attractive, spiritually compelling, proof-positive lifestyles, what good are our claims and pronouncements about a life-changing God?

What we said then, we believe even more now. And that is this: without practically attractive, spiritually compelling, proof-positive lifestyles, what good are our claims and pronouncements about a life-changing God? If we can't outlive the world at every point—in our marriages, with our children, at work, with money, in our relationships, in the use of our time—why dare to speak of salvation and the abundant life? Incarnation of the Word must precede and empower the proclamation of the Word.

Changing lifestyles, therefore, became our driving big idea in those early days. Our preaching focused on it, our small groups practiced it, our training classes encouraged it. In time, we also embellished and enhanced it. You could say our lifestyle idea evolved to the next level. Specifically, we chose to break this Christian lifestyle down into six distinguishing characteristics:

- *Passionately committed to Jesus Christ* (a heart for God)
- *Biblically measured* (everything by the Book)
- *Morally pure* (in a morally compromised age)
- *Family centered* (healthy homes are priority)
- *Evangelistically bold* (willing and confident in sharing one's faith)
- *Socially responsible* (the community around us is our business)

Of course, this emphasis on lifestyle was and is constantly being challenged—by divorce, fear, immorality, threats, legalism, disputes. By the need to be liked. By the desire to be successful. By the never-ending growth we have experienced and the never-ending issues that come with it. The list could go on and on. Our path was, by choice, never easy or safe. But our shared desire for real life and real faith gave us the necessary momentum to move forward.

And like a Polaroid photo developing, we could begin to see the edges around what we hoped to be the Big Picture. Still, it would take several more years before it would come into a clear—and unsettling—focus.

ADDING JOHN 3:16

Many times a great achievement looks, at first, like a terrible mistake. In 1989, more than a decade into our history, Fellowship Bible Church made the startling discovery briefly mentioned in chapter 1. Members of the church, *especially* those committed to authentic spirituality and Christian lifestyles, were feeling increasingly stagnant. After years of growth and personal change, they reported a growing uneasiness. Now that they were all dressed up, just where *were* they supposed to go?

In looking back, we can now see that it was a natural, if terribly disruptive, evolution of a growing spiritual maturity. If our church people were not continually hungering for more, they would likely have felt satiated, not restless. Unless radical action was taken, our dream of being the church Jesus spoke about in the New Testament was in danger. We returned once more to the original mission statement (the big idea) driving us. We all agreed it needed further adjustments. It was not that "equipping Christians to live lifestyles of spiritual integrity" was wrong. It was simply *not enough!* Therefore, in 1990, the mandate to "equip the saints" was divided into two segments:

- Equipping for life
- Equipping for service

To the influence of lifestyles we now incorporated the influence of good works. Our mission statement was soon redrafted to read:

> We exist to manifest the reality of Christ to the world by equipping Christians to live lifestyles of spiritual integrity, which are . . .
>
> - Passionately committed to Jesus Christ
> - Biblically measured
> - Morally pure
> - Family centered
> - Evangelistically bold
> - Socially responsible
>
> . . . and to equip Christians for influential works of service in our community and the world.

All this brought about a significant alteration in the structure of Fellowship Bible Church, which will be discussed in practical detail in chapters 4 and 5. The Big Idea, still coming into focus, was driving the change—an idea with a life of its own, which moved and breathed and, like a wild and brilliant child, was looking for a disciplined freedom. It was the idea that the church should be and must be, at the core, a compelling force of influence—first in lifestyle, then in good works.

Our effort at good works was haphazard at first. For more than five years we labored at this twofold objective, primarily within the confines of the church. More staff were hired, especially pastors to keep a close personal connection between people and leadership. Our growth, though not explosive, was steady and continuous. But our investment in people—in their lifestyles and in helping them find creative outlets of service for their gifts and abilities—started to show a promising return.

Our vision of good works was open-handed: Wherever your gifts and abilities could make a difference for Jesus Christ . . . then go!

Our vision for good works was simple. Help people discover their unique design and then dream with them about where that design could be employed to both stir their passion and advance the kingdom of God. We did not limit our agenda to the usual slots of church need: Sunday school teachers, ushers, helpers in administration, youth workers, musicians. Our vision of good works was openhanded: Wherever your gifts and abilities could make a difference for Jesus Christ . . . then *go!* We will encourage you, support you, serve you, and cheer for you. Go and make a difference!

And much to our joy, people did. While some went inside the church to shore up areas needing improvement, many chose to go outside, into the community. Some joined the efforts of needy nonprofit agencies. Some went to assist the public schools their children were attending. Some went overseas. Some got involved in social issues in government. Some helped start new churches. Some became spiritual mentors. Some started whole new spiritual enterprises: with the poor, with those suffering divorce, with AIDS patients, in prisons. An adoption agency was established; television commercials were produced; the deaf community was reached; and inner-city programs were started.

IRRESISTIBLE INFLUENCE: i²

The Big Idea had grown, but it still remained unruly and not, as yet, fully defined. Leadership sought to channel the excitement it stimulated. We continued to wrestle with the issues it created in order to fully release this power of influence we were learning to appreciate.

At a leadership retreat in the winter of 1996, we carefully attempted to assess the health of our church. Our Big Idea was about to reach its defining moment. Certainly, as most churches go, we had become "successful." From a handful of people in 1977, we now had over 3,500 involved and attending weekly. We had helped plant fifteen additional churches, all of which were healthy and growing. We had been in a continuous building expansion for over ten years. People were being equipped. New ministries were being started. It was all going so well.

But then someone raised a haunting question: "Is our community really being changed?" Was our success mostly an internal barometer or a penetrating reality?

In the wake of reflections and comments that followed, someone read the words of Jesus in Matthew 5:16: "Let your light shine before men, that they may see your good deeds and praise your Father in heaven."

It was as if a floodgate had been lifted. A rush of affirmation followed:

"Now, *that's* influence!" someone said.

"That's the kind of church I would like us to become!" said another.

"That's a vision I could give the rest of my life to!" I said.

Our excitement at this moment transcended the equipping process in which we had labored for almost twenty years. On the wings of a holy moment, launched by the reading of a single verse of Scripture, a *greater vision* took air. We all hungered in this moment to be a church that incarnated the gospel so well and so effectively that our city—rather than scoffing or ridiculing our proclamations, or worse, ignoring us altogether—would, instead, because of our good works, literally feel compelled to give glory to the God they saw working through us.

> **W**e all hungered to be a church that incarnated the gospel so well and so effectively that our city would literally feel compelled to give glory to the God they saw working through us.

More dangerous dreaming about the church.

"What that is," said Bill Wellons, one of our teaching pastors, "is Jesus' idea of irresistible influence!"

"i², " I said spontaneously.

i²—a bridge over the troubled waters between an isolated church and a cynical culture.

A bridge where credibility could be reestablished by God's people before an increasingly skeptical and hostile world. A bridge where people would be drawn to cross over, rather than be repelled. A bridge of proof, rather than hollow proclamation. A bridge of incarnation: the dynamic intersection of the divine and the human.

In that holy moment we could all see it, shining like the majestic Golden Gate in late evening light, a thing of incalculable beauty and grace: a bridge of irresistible influence.

SHOOTING FOR THE MOON

In my next "State of the Church" address in 1997, just months after landing on i², I spoke of President John F. Kennedy's radical challenge to the nation in 1961. Earlier that year the Soviet Union had shocked the world by sending the first man into space. One month later America followed with a fifteen-minute space flight by Alan Sheppard aboard Friendship I. Everyone was excited, but it only marked a beginning. On September 12, 1961, President John F. Kennedy made a bold, almost unbelievable announcement, calling every American to a noble idea many would think impossible: "We choose to go to the moon. We choose to go to the moon in this decade, not because it is easy, but because it is hard!"

In time, Kennedy's bold idea captured America's imagination, will, priorities, a good portion of the national budget, and its brightest and best people. But it also did something else for America. It created new heroes, new frontiers, and feats of incredible courage. It caused our country to focus on an ambition greater than ourselves. It brought us moments of breathtaking glory. Who can forget those heart-stopping words, "Houston, the Eagle has landed."

The church of irresistible influence. The church of i². A great idea!

For our church, i² was shooting for the moon. A bold—and, some would say, impossible—idea to propel Fellowship Bible Church into the twenty-first century and compel us beyond our superficial successes. An idea larger than more buildings and more people and more programs for ourselves. An idea to capture the imagination, will, money, talents, and resources of each and every person. An idea whose execution would be difficult and dangerous but would spawn heroes, feats of courage, and moments of glory for God's kingdom.

The church of irresistible influence. The church of i². A great idea!

"I want us to choose to pursue being this kind of church," I told our congregation. "Not because it is easy, but because it too is hard. It is the proof our world desperately needs before it will ever seriously consider our truth."

I then quoted Matthew 5:16 and broke it down into phrases to explain:

"Jesus is telling us to take what he has done for you and in you . . . take that **light** . . . *and what it has done to transform your lives, your abilities, your resources* . . . and use it **in such a way** . . . *which speaks to strategy, a strategy that draws people rather than repels them* . . . **that they** . . . *meaning the world around us, our friends, our neighborhoods, our city, even our state* . . . **may see our good works** . . . *not endure our haughty arrogance, not suffer through more of our unsupported boasts, not react again to our mean-spirited remarks—no!—see our good works* . . . and because of that undeniable goodness, because of those humble works of love, our community, rather than ignoring, ridiculing, or reacting in unnecessary anger, would instead do something absolutely amazing: **Give glory to our Father who is in Heaven!**"

That message was four years ago. Today our church has moved forward and flourishes under the banner of this compelling idea. It has done exactly what great ideas do: it has challenged us to be more than a club. It has pushed us beyond the self-satisfying borders of success. It has pressed, rallied, and organized us to work at, pray for, and measure ourselves by a much higher and weightier standard: influence. The kind of radical influence Jesus talked about. The kind that makes for peace, not war. The kind that serves, not shouts. The kind that draws admiration, not a reaction. The kind that connects with unbelievers, inspiring them to the point of actually drawing praise from their lips.

Few people at Fellowship Bible Church feel stagnant or bored any more—not since we have embraced this higher calling of bridge building. Today opportunities and construction are everywhere. And we are seeing steps of faith, feats of courage, and spiritual initiatives in the lives of our members that would have been unimaginable just a few years ago.

It has been quite an evolution. And the root of it all lies in a simple idea birthed from the mind of Jesus himself—i².

BRIDGE BUILDER QUESTIONS

What is the "big idea" defining and driving your church?

Could your church be accurately described as "a club"? If the answer is no, why not?

Is your church a stranger to your community?

CHAPTER 4

THE CORE OF i² CONSTRUCTION

If you build it, they will come . . .

—the movie, *Field of Dreams*

A BRIDGE STORY

In May of 1845, the Wheeling Intelligencer *published a vivid account of the collapse of Charles Ellet's suspension bridge over the Ohio River just five years after completion. A portion of the article read:*

About 3 o'clock yesterday we walked toward the Suspension Bridge and went upon it, as we have frequently done, enjoying a cool breeze and the undulating motion of the bridge. . . . We had been off the flooring only two minutes, and were on Main Street when we saw persons running toward the river bank; we followed just in time to see the whole structure heaving and dashing with tremendous force.

For a few minutes we watched it with breathless anxiety, lunging like a ship in a storm; at one time it rose to nearly the height of the tower, then fell, and twisted and writhed, and was dashed almost bottom upward. At last there seemed to be a determined twist along the entire span, about one half of the flooring being nearly reversed, and down went the immense structure from its dizzy height to the stream below, with an appalling crash and roar. . . .

We witnessed the terrific scene. The great body of flooring and the suspenders, forming something like a basket swung between two towers, was swayed to and fro like the motion of a pendulum. Each vibration giving it increased momentum, the cables, which sustained the whole structure, were unable to resist a force operating on them in so many different directions, and were literally twisted and wrenched from their fastenings.[1]

In the pioneering years of bridge building, spectacular collapses were not unusual. In her book, Bridges, Judith Dupre writes, "By the end of the nineteenth century, with the expansion of the railroad, bridge collapses were noted with increasing regularity and hysteria."[2]

Bridges involve complicated engineering, delicately and powerfully balancing the often competing physics of tension, compression, shear, and torsion. Most bridge disasters, therefore, have one thing in common: errors in engineering.

THE APPOINTMENT IS ON my calendar: a meeting with the mayors of Little Rock and North Little Rock. Despite their own busy schedules, they have graciously offered to drive out to our church for an engagement only vaguely described to them.

Less than five years ago I would probably have received a polite refusal on official stationery written by an assistant, or at best maybe a brief appointment as a courtesy or civic duty—at *their* office.

But today these mayors *believe*. It's not that they necessarily embrace our theology, our ideology, or our values. But we are no longer a mystery, a threat, or an undesirable element that has to be tolerated. They know us! And what they believe is that our church is a real asset to the community, worthy of their time and attention. They have embraced us as a positive contributor and philanthropic partner. And for a church, that is no small feat.

An important bridge has been built. For more than ten years, people from our church have slowly moved into our community with love and charity, establishing preschool programs, literacy assistance, friendship clubs, summer camps, even college scholarship funding. These mayors have seen proof positive.

They have witnessed our community "Family Forums," which we offer at hotels, business conference rooms, and hospitals. They have read the newspaper ads that appear each fall, calling the men of our city to join with us in a yearlong quest for a nobler masculinity called "Men's Fraternity." They have seen us hold yearly celebrations at a water theme park honoring city employees—police officers and their families, firefighters, and local schoolteachers. They have participated in our Racial Reconciliation Rally that drew 15,000 people at Riverfront Park. They have partnered with us on city "work days" for four consecutive years, in the last three of which we mobilized more than a thousand volunteers. Through these positive connections and more, these mayors believe. Why?

Seeing . . . is believing.

THAT WHICH WE HAVE SEEN, TOUCHED, AND HEARD

The apostle John was emphatic about this same concrete reality in Jesus—his tangible, earthly, physical presence. In 1 John 1:1–2, look at the number of times he refers to the palpability of Christ:

That which was from the beginning, which we have *heard,* which we have *seen* with our eyes, which we have *looked at* and our hands *have touched*—this we proclaim concerning the Word of life. The life *appeared;* we have *seen* it and testify to it, and we proclaim to you the eternal life, which was with the Father and has *appeared* to us.

Again and again John purposely appeals to the human senses for proof positive. Why? Because a spiritual bridge always involves a physical reality. People need to see to believe.

Did you ever wonder why God simply did not wave a magic wand to accomplish salvation and the reality of a full and eternal life? Couldn't he have just said the divine equivalent of *abracadabra,* and all would be well? Apparently not.

> *A spiritual bridge always involves a physical reality. People need to see to believe.*

Bridging chasms between people demands a tangible reality too. Touch, taste, smell, hearing, and sight are intricately involved. Contact is both the means and the goal. Love is highly sensory.

Unfortunately for the community, the church has become practically invisible in this regard. Secluded and huddled together, the body of Christ might be fairly described by the world as that "which we have *not seen* with our eyes, which we have *not looked at,* and our hands have *not touched.*"

When I first approached our church about the concept of irresistible influence, our connections with our community were at best sporadic—a few dangling wires loosely and tenuously attached to the other side of the Great Chasm. So how did we move from a position of estrangement from our community to that of being embraced by mayors? Where does this road less traveled begin that leads to the irresistible influence Jesus envisioned? We have found that i² construction demands three significant ingredients—irreducible minimums, if you will: confession, vision, and structure.

(1) Confession: The Starting Point

Confession is the starting point for any i² construction. We must painfully and with great sorrow admit that the flimsy efforts we pass off as bridges are not really bridges at all. They are so much hot air and, as such, are as insubstantial as clouds or dreams. The true measures of a church are not "how many" but "how *loving,*" not "how relevant" but "how *real.*"

Confession means reading afresh the words of Jesus Christ about his concept of the church—"salt" and "light"—and being grief stricken over how far our churches fall short. It's hearing the warnings of modern critics like church strategist Michael Regele, who says, "If we don't reform ourselves to the places we live in, we will continue to disconnect and, ultimately, will disconnect right out of existence."[3]

> *Confession means reading afresh the words of Jesus Christ about his concept of the church—"salt" and "light"—and being grief stricken over how far our churches fall short.*

We need to confess this undeniable shortfall and weep. Yes, *weep!* Heartfelt confession is a healthy and necessary starting place for the evangelical church today. We must admit to ourselves our ever-declining impact on the culture. "Incredibly," writes George Barna, "most Christians don't perceive the church to be in the most severe struggle it has faced in centuries."[4]

Desperation and regret are the precursors of a new vision. If there is any hope to span the Great Chasm with a radical i2 blueprint, it will first be revealed through confession.

I am reminded of such a moment in the Old Testament when the Word of God was rediscovered—at least in meaning. That moment occurred during the time of Ezra and Nehemiah when Israel was trying to rebuild both its capitol and its identity after seventy long and desperate years of Babylonian captivity. Here's what happened:

> When the seventh month came and the Israelites had settled in their towns, all the people assembled as one man in the square before the Water Gate. They told Ezra the scribe to bring out the Book of the Law of Moses, which the LORD had commanded for Israel. . . . Ezra opened the book. All the people could see him because he was standing above them; and as he opened it, the people all stood up. Ezra praised the LORD, the great God and all the people lifted their hands and responded, "Amen! Amen!" Then they bowed down and worshiped the LORD with their faces to the ground. The Levites . . . instructed

the people in the Law while the people were standing there. They read from the Book of the Law of God, making it clear and giving the meaning so that the people could understand what was being read. (Nehemiah 8:1, 5–8)

That last phrase is particularly important. Ezra and his companions didn't just read the Scripture; they helped the people *understand* it. The people got in touch with its radical pronouncements about direction and lifestyle. And, how did the hearers react? Nehemiah 8:9 states that Nehemiah said, "This day is sacred to the LORD your God. Do not mourn or weep." It goes on to say, "For all the people had been weeping as they listened to the words of the Law."

These people finally understood that their problems were not in bullies like the Babylonians or in circumstances like the broken walls of a defenseless Jerusalem. *They* were the problem! The fault was in who they were and how they were living.

It is impossible to overstate the significance of this moment of penetrating conviction. But their tears of grief certainly illustrate it. Later, all Israel gathered to hear just how far off track the whole nation was from God's original blueprint:

On the twenty-fourth day of the same month, the Israelites gathered together, fasting and wearing sackcloth and having dust on their heads. Those of Israelite descent had separated themselves from all foreigners. They stood in their places and confessed their sins and the wickedness of their fathers. They stood where they were and read from the Book of the Law of the LORD their God for a quarter of the day, and spent another quarter in confession and in worshiping the LORD their God. (Nehemiah 9:1–3)

And what did they confess? They confessed their wrong direction, their misplaced priorities, their pride, and the enormous compromises that had settled comfortably into their lifestyles. But their tears of confession before the Word of God also became something powerful: it became a defining moment for courageous *change*.

Remember, until one senses a desperate loss, there is little motivation for radical alteration. And radical alteration is the core issue for the church as it transitions into the twenty-first century. It must be a radical alteration that goes beyond style that updates the church's image. It must be one of substance that transforms the life of the church and causes it to once again become a force of moral power and earthshaking influence in its community.

So let us confess that our comfort, our moral compromises, and our misguided pursuits and priorities have rendered us increasingly impotent before the watching world. Only when we are desperately regretful of our current condition is there any hope at all for reconsidering how to span the Great Chasm.

(2) Vision: Seeing What God Wants Us to Be

Real vision, of course, is seeing what God clearly wants us to be. And through the grid of a New Testament blueprint, the idea of being or remaining a church "club" or church "success story" becomes noxious. In seeking to become a church of irresistible influence, church leaders must again, in practical terms, envision for their people the church as profiled by Jesus and the apostles within the pages of the New Testament:

- A church passionately committed to Jesus Christ and to the proclamation of the gospel;
- A church of winsome lifestyles punctuated by high moral standards;
- A church of radical love and selfless good deeds that amazes the world around it.

> *Through the grid of a New Testament blueprint, the idea of being or remaining a church "club" or a church "success story" becomes noxious.*

This is the church of the New Testament: a church that loves its enemies rather than mocking them (Romans 12:17–21); a church that gives more than it receives (Acts 20:35); a church that moves courageously "out" rather than retreating comfortably "in" and in that process proves its authenticity (Matthew 5:16).

This New Testament vision must find its way back into our congregations!

When I first introduced the vision of i² to our church, it was after years of uninterrupted

growth for our church. Our people were actively serving and supporting one another. Our facilities and staff were constantly expanding.
More people were coming. In many ways, we were like the successful
businessman who had accomplished in half a life more than he ever
imagined in a whole one. And yet the haunting question for him—and
us—was, Now what? Should we plan on "more of the same"? Should
we keep expanding through an endless cycle of building, growing,
building, growing? Or should we consider a different path?

Over the easier option of an ever-expanding institutionalism, we
chose instead to pursue the more challenging biblical vision of influence. Practically, that immediately translated into three major decisions,
resulting in specific and dramatic changes:

- We chose to finish our church campus and halt our never-ending construction. This meant the church facility we now have,
  with its fairly balanced distribution of worship, education, and
  office space, would be *used* more but would not significantly
  grow more.
- We chose to eliminate all debt so we could help maximize our
  ability to give large amounts of money and resources away.
- We chose to hire "specialty staff" who could help us maximize
  our bridge-building efforts to the community through strategic
  initiatives. These new staff members would be community-
  focused, not church-focused.

New Testament vision caused us to begin this courageous reconstruction process. It also led us to radically embrace influence as our priority and growth as merely a by-product, rather than visa versa. In doing
so, it changed everything—especially how we actually do church.

(3) Structure: Unleashing People with Purpose

Vision—no matter how in line with the vision of Jesus—is never
enough. Execution of the vision is what counts. And execution, to a
large degree, depends on structure. With its structure, every church succeeds or fails. Preachers often have difficulty with this statement because
structure seems so, well, "unspiritual." It's not. Perhaps the time-tested
wisdom of Peter Drucker can be of some help here:

Brilliant men are often strikingly ineffectual; they fail to realize that the brilliant insight is not by itself achievement. They never have learned that insights become effectiveness only through hard, systematic work. . . . Intelligence, imagination, and knowledge are essential resources, but only effectiveness converts them into results.[5]

With its structure, every church succeeds or fails.

Brilliant ideas spill from thousands of pulpits every Sunday, destined for a quick, premature death. Why? Because only structure, well-thought-out structure, which effectively unleashes people with purpose, can get results.

Developing an effective structure, of course, is a tremendously difficult task, balancing the seemingly opposite needs of stability and flexibility. As in bridge building, err on either side and you have a catastrophe in the making. If you make structure overly rigid, the system can become a tyranny of task, a series of stiff and oppressive duties. If you make structure too flexible, it is likely to be torn apart by the movement of uneducated and undisciplined good intentions.

Church structure is always a difficult discussion. There is no "one size fits all" kind of structure; each church must bridge a unique environment and culture, one that needs to be in constant evolution according to the forces acting upon it. Nevertheless, over the last twenty years, we have found that there *are* some general but essential structural concepts that should be considered for any church in an i^2 pursuit.

In reconstructing Fellowship Bible Church with i^2 blueprints, three of these structural concepts have prevailed. The i^2 church must be structured for:

- hands-on i^2 exposures
- personal i^2 ministry
- strategic i^2 investments

These three elements, built into an equilibrium of flexibility and support, have provided our church with the necessary structure for building bridges into our world.

HANDS-ON i² EXPOSURES

Hands-on i² exposures are, by definition, carefully selected church projects that allow uninitiated church members the opportunity to cross over and successfully interact with the community.

Clearly, one of the greatest roadblocks to i² construction lies in convincing a congregation that such a bridge *can* be built. A majority of churchgoers have become practical atheists in this regard. Their mindset is that this world is an irredeemable lost cause. You can even quote them Proverbs 11:11: "Through the blessing of the upright a city is exalted"; or you can remind them that history tells us of how whole communities were turned upside down by the faith of a few.

"Maybe back then," they will mumble, but not in today's world with its pluralistic attitudes, sanctioned immoralities, and encouraged disbelief. Many speak of "the world" in much the same way—with equally paired stresses—as a farmer hisses out the phrase: "rootworm." Something awful. Something to be avoided.

To overcome this inbred disgust of the world, we must creatively, strategically, and carefully reintroduce our people to it. "Exposure" is the operative word here, which means providing church members with specific opportunities to connect with the world in a way that will build both confidence and compassion.

For instance, our congregation was surprised at the goodwill created between ourselves and city government when we partnered with them in "Helping Hands," a project I mentioned in chapter 2. Everyone benefited from this partnership: New lines of communication were opened and friendships built, the city was helped practically, and yes—some people in the ensuing interaction were saved spiritually.

But the greatest blessing was how this firsthand exposure of working with our city altered the thinking of our people. Suddenly the city and its leaders were no longer strangers. They were real people with real needs that we could relate to, pray for, and interact with. When a bridge connects, nothing can stay the same.

> *"Exposure"* means providing church members with specific opportunities to connect with the world in a way that will build both confidence and compassion.

Several years ago, our church "adopted" an inner-city housing project called Eastgate. It became a way for our mostly white church to touch a part of the community that is so easy to ignore, to complain about, or to fear. Over the last twelve years, hundreds of our youth and adults have had the opportunity to teach reading-readiness programs, serve as mentors, form friendship clubs, lead Bible studies, and coach sports teams through a highly organized program called STEP (Serving To Equip People). Through STEP, scores of inner-city youth have found a new life in Jesus Christ.

Three of these youth—Sanchee Gate, Travis Jackson, and Karen Williams—recently stood before our transfixed congregation and, with tears, recounted how their years in the STEP ministry not only transformed their lives but provided for them what otherwise would have been an unthinkable next step: college.

But as life-changing and hope-inspiring as STEP has been for these young people, this kind of exposure makes an even greater impact on our church body. It shakes off some of our disbelief about "the world." It shows us that the community, even the inner-city community, can be bridged.

Whether it is an ongoing program such as STEP, or partnering as we did with the American Red Cross to fill its dangerously low blood banks, or working with city officials on projects important to them, the point is this: *Church leadership must structure these i^2 exposures into church life and onto church calendars.* In doing so, leaders will:

- Constantly challenge an otherwise convenient mindset of retreat;
- Break down harmful stereotypes and fear;
- Demonstrate outreach as a church priority;
- Model to the congregation *how* to spiritually engage the community in a positive way;
- Affirm these kinds of efforts as "spiritual";
- Unleash a new kind of thinking among its church members— theologically, socially, and experientially;
- Build goodwill in the overall community.

The church must be *led* into the world. In the new light of exposure, people begin to recognize the vital importance of building bridges. They not only know it, but they also feel it.

PERSONAL i² MINISTRY

A second concept for i² construction is the formation of a structure that unleashes an intentional process known as personal i² ministry. In terms of impact, first on church members and later on the surrounding community, this process is at the heart of i². *Process* is the key word.

Most churches group people into Sunday school classes or small groups for the purpose of providing spiritual growth and social connections. Unfortunately, these groupings often end up as perpetual "holding tanks" where Christians become increasingly comfortable with each other and themselves, and increasingly disconnected from our world.

Our small group ministry, known as "Community Groups," suffered this same fate in the late 1980s. As mentioned before, our members expressed a growing disenchantment after four or five years with the small group ministry we had created to provide for them a sense of intimacy and interaction. Since our small group ministry represents the core and lifeblood of Fellowship Bible Church, this was no small issue.

The problem was that growing and learning together in these small group environments was simply not enough to sustain a vital spiritual life. Why? Because in the journey of spiritual life, one matures fully, not just with growing and learning, but with serving.

The Christian life is intended to crescendo around each person finding his or her place in . . . kingdom work.

The Christian life is intended to crescendo around each person finding his or her place in the constantly unfolding fabric of kingdom work that engages the unique gifts and abilities with which each person has been endowed by God (1 Peter 4:10–11). Structures that ignore or merely pay occasional lip service to the development of this critical element of the Christian life will, in time, find their people bored, restless—or worse, stagnant. The glory of spiritual adventure departs, and filling the void becomes self-centeredness, entertainment, comfort, endless events and programming, and a host of other lesser things.

To counteract this, Fellowship Bible Church created a small group structure that intentionally processes people toward finding a personal ministry of influence. It can be diagrammed as follows:

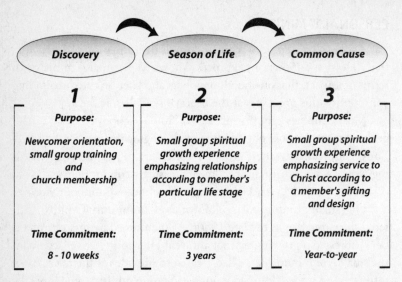

Discovery is the assimilation ministry of Fellowship. It welcomes newcomers, orients them to the church, and readies those who are willing to join the church for their first small group experience. The process begins with Discovery I, a one-session orientation class. It serves to tell the dynamic story of Fellowship Bible Church through a video history and live staff testimonies. The vision of the church is described in detail as well as the essential nature of small groups to the mission of the church. Everyone is told up front that over time Fellowship is designed to move individuals like themselves to a place of personal and passionate ministry. Indeed, this is the primary work of the church. Our success or failure will be measured by this ultimate objective.

Participants are then invited to take the next step, Discovery II, which takes eight weeks. Here, individuals make commitments necessary to become members of Fellowship Bible Church, while also receiving small group training. In some cases, the small group that will support these new members over the coming years is actually formed during Discovery II with the help of our staff.

Following Discovery II, everyone selects one of Fellowship's **Season of Life** congregations and joins one of that congregation's designated small groups. It is important to note that each of these congregations addresses a specific life stage: single adults, young married, middle-aged couples, empty nesters, and so on. Each is served by a vocational pastor, and each is broken into small groups led by a trained layperson or couple. The following diagram will help visualize this:

Fellowship's Season of Life Congregations

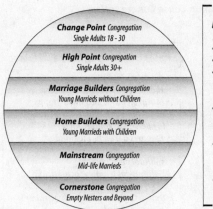

Change Point Congregation
Single Adults 18 - 30

High Point Congregation
Single Adults 30+

Marriage Builders Congregation
Young Marrieds without Children

Home Builders Congregation
Young Marrieds with Children

Mainstream Congregation
Mid-life Marrieds

Cornerstone Congregation
Empty Nesters and Beyond

Each Season of Life Congregation:

• Is life stage specific
• Is directed by a pastoral leader
• Is broken down into small groups of 12-14 people and led by a trained lay person or couple
• Employs a specific Bible-based curriculum for members' spiritual development
• Emphasizes relational connectedness for personal encouragement and accountability
• Equips participant in the i² philosophy of the church

The Season of Life experience seeks to ground each participant in a healthy spiritual life through a spiritually centered curriculum. It also helps connect people to one another in meaningful and vital relationships while equipping each member philosophically to the church's vision of i².

Probably the most unique feature about these Seasons of Life congregations is that they are *time-oriented*. Each Season of Life small group experience lasts for three years and then one must move on! No "holding tanks" here—just more adventure! After three years of being relationally connected, spiritually grounded, and philosophically equipped, the next phase is toward finding one's usefulness in the kingdom of God.

We call this transition, "graduating" into **Common Cause**. This congregation, like the others, is broken down into lay-led small groups that also employ various kinds of Bible studies for their members' spiritual development. But rather than form around a specific season of life, these small groups are formed for a *specific service* and last only one year.

Some groups serve needs within the church, while others serve causes outside the church either in the community or in areas around the world. At the end of each year, members either recommit to another year of service in that specific area or use that experience to better focus the use of their gifts elsewhere.

Fellowship's Common Cause Congregation

Small Groups
serving needs in the church

Small Groups
serving needs in the community

Small Groups
serving needs around the world

Our Common Cause Congregation:

• Is ministry specific
• Is directed by a team of pastoral leaders
• Is broken down into small groups of 12-14 people and led by a trained lay person or couple
• Employs a specific Bible-based curriculum for members' ongoing spiritual development
• Emphasizes a highly focused area of service with clear objectives that actively employs each member's gifts and abilites
• Equips members to ultimately find his or her unique place in serving the Kingdom of God.

As I write this, we are once again experiencing our annual spring graduation. Approximately three hundred people are making the transition from Seasons of Life to Common Cause. Over a thousand people will now make up this growing congregation, broken into more than eighty service groups. Here is just a partial list of some of this year's Common Cause groups that will be connecting with our community:

BETHANY CHRISTIAN SERVICES SUPPORT: Offering support to an organization committed to being a resource for adoption and promoting Bethany's services to the community, including coordination of an annual fund-raising banquet.

CELEBRATE RECOVERY: Group provides worship and small group ministry support to those in the community seeking freedom from hurts, hang-ups, and life-threatening addictions.

CHRISTIAN EDUCATIONAL ASSISTANCE FOUNDATION (CEAF) SUPPORT: Provides support to activities of a foundation providing scholarships to low-income families desiring a Christian education.

COMMUNITY IMPACT NETWORK: Matching community needs with the formation of new Common Cause groups, providing training and encouragement to these groups and other churches.

CRISIS PREGNANCY CENTER SUPPORT: Seeking to save lives and promote the gospel by offering support, counseling, and baby-care classes to expectant mothers facing critical decisions.

CROWN MINISTRY: Encouraging good stewardship and a stronger relationship with God through the teaching of biblical principles of financial responsibility.

DEAF MINISTRY: Caring for deaf individuals through Bible teaching, Christian fellowship, and opportunities for service.

DISASTER FOLLOW-UP: Networking individuals with local assistance agencies in the wake of natural disasters and ministering to their needs in practical ways.

DIVORCE CARE: Working with individuals in healing and reentry into life after their divorce. Facilitates ongoing seminars and support groups throughout the year.

DIVORCE PREVENTION: Offers a thirteen-week seminar and individual attention to couples contemplating divorce in the hope of reviving troubled marriages.

HABITAT FOR HUMANITY: Constructing homes for the underprivileged, recruiting workers from our church and other churches, and developing relationships with the families for whom the homes are built.

HELPING HANDS: Developing the foundation for the "Tithe-A-Day" program for churches throughout central Arkansas to utilize in creating and implementing similar service days to benefit their community.

HONDURAS MISSIONS SUPPORT: Supporting Fellowship's missions outreach in the country of Honduras, promoting missions work in the congregation, and assisting the various missions agencies with which we partner in Honduras.

JOBS PARTNERSHIP: Facilitates partnerships between churches and businesses in the community to help individuals who struggle to keep meaningful employment.

LIFE SKILLS/MEDICAL: Facilitates relationships connecting seasoned and successful physicians with younger medical students.

LTCare SUPPORT: Providing logistical and directional advisory support to the Love-Truth-Care ministry in its food distribution and inner-city community development efforts.

MINISTRY TO INNER-CITY CHILDREN: Facilitates annual fund-raisers to send inner-city children to Christian summer camps and to offer college scholarships to promising underprivileged students in the community.

NEARLY-WED/NEWLYWED MENTORS: Recruiting, training, and mobilizing mentors to draw alongside pre-married/early-married couples in order for the marriages at Fellowship to be strong and healthy in the future.

NURSING HOME SUPPORT: Provides services that will help in meeting the spiritual, social, and physical needs of elderly citizens in both nursing and rehabilitation facilities as well as in private homes.

ONE-TO-ONE EVANGELISM: Seeking special opportunities in the community to connect with people in order to share the Good News of Jesus Christ.

OPEN HANDS: Sharing physical, spiritual, and emotional support with single parents, the needy, and the elderly in the church community.

PUBLIC SCHOOLS MENTORING: Supporting the EXCEL abstinence program at an area junior high school, mentoring students and partnering with them as they make the choice for abstinence in the face of peer pressure.

SPORTSMEN'S QUEST: Develops and models evangelistic ministries around hunting/fishing activities in the community for single parents or mentors and children.

STUDENT VENTURE GROUP: Offering evangelistic and discipleship outreach to a junior and senior high school in the community, building relationships with young people and modeling life in Christ.

UPWARD BASKETBALL: Provides leadership and resources to facilitate an annual eight-week evangelistic basketball program to the unchurched in our community.

These "trial-and-error," year-to-year experiences in a Common Cause small group can be frustrating, exhilarating, too broad, too narrow, incredible, impotent, eye-opening, exhausting, empowering—or in some cases, all of the above! But, through this intentional process, people are challenged and stretched while discovering what they enjoy and are good at. Christianity becomes a continuing adventure, just as it was designed to be. And we have found that in time, through this process, many people finally connect with a spiritual cause they are passionate about. And passion changes everything.

The transition to Common Cause is a critical one for members of our church. After their Season of Life experience, they know people; they know the church; they know its vision and i² direction. Now it's time to decide how they, with their unique gifts and abilities, can make a significant contribution to God's kingdom.

Even though we have a clear process for helping them through this transition (described in the next chapter), graduating from Seasons of Life is much like graduating from college. It's scary. It forces upon each graduate a crisis of purpose. *But, that's so healthy!* To stay in college may feel safe, but the truth is that in time such a choice will corrupt life, not further it. Spiritual "holding tanks" do the same. That's why it is necessary to move people on. At some point, the questions must be asked: What is the spiritual purpose of my life? Where has God designed me to serve? I believe church structure must help people ask those critical questions, and then answer them.

Let me remind you, the key word in all this is *structure*. Structure serves as a way of channeling, not damming up, a person's purpose of skillfully serving others in love. Our structure at Fellowship Bible Church is not perfect or permanent (we are constantly refining it), but *it is intentional.* With it, people move through a specific process to personal i^2 ministry.

STRATEGIC i^2 INVESTMENTS

Finally, i^2 construction demands the church be structured for strategic i^2 investments. What do I mean by that?

At some point, the questions must be asked: What is the spiritual purpose of my life? Where has God designed me to serve? I believe church structure must help people ask those critical questions, and then answer them.

If your church has a missions program, you already have a form of this structure. Your church has determined by one process or another to invest people and dollars in some region of the world where you believe you can make a difference.

Strategic i^2 investments, however, are not necessarily overseas. They can, in fact, be anywhere. The key word is *strategic,* meaning that every church must have a way of determining what "strategic" is for itself. It must also possess a structure for maximizing its influence in those areas.

For instance, early on Fellowship Bible Church determined that planting new, vibrant churches was one of our strategic callings. In the early days, our efforts at planting new churches consisted of simply breaking off a small portion of our own membership, giving them our blessing and a little cash, and then hoping for the best.

But now we have developed a reliable church-planting process so that our new church plants have proven, reliable tracks to follow. We also provide consultation and support to the leaders of these new churches through the availability of some of our senior staff.

Just recently we have taken an even more aggressive step. We have now created a small company whose focus, in part, is to train some of the next generation of pastoral leaders through a church-based Leadership Residency Program. Each year this company recruits several of the top seminary graduates in the country to come to Little Rock to engage in a one-year leadership training program at Fellowship Bible Church.

All this, we believe, will help advance one of our strategic i² invest-ments—the establishment of healthy, vibrant churches across our state and nation. We have chosen to make it one of our church's highest pri-orities. Every church, of course, should think long and carefully about its own strategic mission, while paying close attention to the needs of its local community. Strategy involves asking a series of tough questions: What are our unique strengths as a church? What are the critical issues of our community? Which of those can our church effectively influ-ence? Do we have a structure that can move our people to those needs? Are we willing to commit resources, staff, and people to make an impact?

Here is a complete list of the strategic i² investment initiatives we adopted as a church after our own careful review:

FELLOWSHIP'S i² INVESTMENTS

- To powerfully connect with our city in philanthropic partnerships;
- To bless our city with more and more strategic Common Cause ministries, which build genuine relationships and open doors for the sharing of the gospel;
- To give significant gifts of money to strategic faith-based causes that minister beyond the reach of Fellowship Bible Church;
- To help train the next generation of pastoral leaders through a church-based Leadership Residency Program;
- To assist large numbers of churches in their development through an annual church training conference;
- To plant and nurture new churches throughout the United States;
- To advance the fulfillment of the Great Commission.

A CHURCH BUILT OUT

Two millennia ago, Jesus Christ interceded for his disciples in prayer. In this holy moment, shortly before he was to die, his final heart cry for them was being poured out to his Father. He requested that these men, in the days ahead, not be taken from the world (John 17:15), but instead, be empowered to move on it and into it. He prayed to his

Father, "As you sent me into the world, I have sent them into the world" (John 17:18). We need to note that prayer also included *us:* "My prayer is not for them alone. I pray also for those who will believe in me through their message" (John 17:20).

To his very end, Jesus was focused on his dream: a church built not only upon truth but one *built out,* like a bridge, into the world. Why? "To let the world know that you sent me" (John 17:23).

Clearly, a new kind of church is needed in the twenty-first century—a church that connects more authentically with the world while allowing the world a better and more effective way to come and connect with it. To cross over. But to get us there will require the hard work of new construction.

I have offered here what I believe are the key ingredients for bringing to life Jesus' dream of a bridge of irresistible influence. It's a work that will require heartfelt confession, bold vision, and in the end, a carefully crafted, well-developed structure that moves churchgoers out of their endless huddles and effectively "into the world."

And if we build it, they will come.

BRIDGE BUILDER QUESTIONS

This chapter states that "the church must be led into the world." In what ways has church leadership provided opportunities for your congregation to be exposed to, and to successfully interact with, your community?

What is the primary purpose of your church structure? How is it designed to process and move people into personal ministry?

What changes in your church structure are critically needed?

CHAPTER 5

FROM LAY SPECTATORS TO i² PARTICIPANTS

A church rooted in the living Lord is a church

that encourages people to move beyond their

comfort zones and invest themselves in face-to-face,

person-to-person, hands-on kinds of ministries.

—George Gallup Jr.

A BRIDGE STORY

Over time and generations, living on an island shapes the way you think and perceive reality. Isolation makes you different by definition, sets you apart. There is, in a highlighted fashion, a greater distance between here *and* there, *and* us *and* them. *It's inevitable. Most islanders, in fact, wouldn't have it any other way. That's why they choose to live on an island.*

Island living is often peaceful, serene, undisturbed, and largely disconnected from the greater span of the real world; it's a carefully measured existence, a way of life.

For centuries residents of Prince Edward Island, off Canada's eastern coast, enjoyed just such an existence. The island was once described as "two huge beaches separated by potato fields." Islanders were distanced from the chaos of the real world by nine miles of ocean. You could not drive there or back.

From the soil of such an unconnected serenity sprung Anne of Green Gables. Red-haired, pigtailed, freckled, and innocent, Anne became a powerful and defining symbol of the island's character. She was also fictional.

Paradoxically, it was Anne's rising fame that attracted outsiders.

In 1997, after a bitter and dividing referendum battle, the Confederation Bridge connecting Prince Edward Island to the mainland of Canada was opened, finally fulfilling the government's 132-year-old promise. The technology of the bridge, which consisted of 185 structural elements, each placed within one-quarter inch accuracy, was stunning. Constructed on land and transported by ship, the bridge cost nearly $1 billion dollars. Many residents say it cost much more.

With the completion of the bridge, the island was suddenly awash with tourists, foreigners to their cherubic, carefully cultivated lifestyle. Tourism doubled. Unsettling, disturbing, and deep changes followed. Near Green Gables, Anne's name is now used to promote dolls, T-shirts, potato chips, a golf course, restaurants, a wax museum, and bungalows. Many residents believe Anne must be rolling over in her fictional grave.

For many of the island's longtime residents, paranoia runs high about what lies in the future. Some are fiercely angry with those they perceive as having sold out. The island's capitalists, however, see new jobs, greater efficiency, and a welcome end to the often interminable waits for the ferry. Those caught in the middle believe they might just as well get used to it.

With the completion of the bridge, only one thing remains certain: the island, for good or bad, will never be the same.

A CHURCH IS OFTEN an island. Not only does it fail to construct bridges to the world, but it doubts even the possibility of such a difficult and costly work. Exiled from its true purpose, the church retreats, focused on programs and good psychology and creating images, all of which are helpful and well-meaning, but are fueled on, and for the purpose of, continuing introspection. These walls of isolation soon turn into mirrors. Church members who desperately need to live lives of purpose have little to look at but each other. Appearances, the collective and personal cultivation of a mostly fictional reality—one in which a literary character such as Anne of Green Gables might have grown up to be the mayor—take on a new importance.

Living in ignorance, the church forgets, like a person slowly surrendering to the onslaught of Alzheimer's, which direction God has called it to pursue. On an island, the church is always lost. Movement, by necessity, is always circular—around itself—and never in the mostly straight line of an ongoing vision from God. Island living is sometimes monotonous, but it is capriciously comfortable and safe, as much as is possible in such a fallen and dangerous world.

> *On an island, the church is always lost.*

Then someone—some well-meaning but dangerous dreamer—has the audacity to introduce a church referendum: to build a bridge. To go out there. All the way *to them!* What's worse, bridges are two-way. *Them* is no longer a carefully constructed composite character of the mind—one that permits a safe, if somewhat cold, distance. *Them,* suddenly, is here, and here can be there. Such a connection will bring with it change, challenges, and yes, conflicts.

Most church people instinctively know: A bridge changes everything.

THE ENDS OF THE CHURCH

Recently I traveled to the ends of the church—our church, that is. Literally. Experientially. Spiritually. The occasion for this journey was a Sunday night where two meetings were occurring simultaneously at opposite locations of our facility. It became, for me, a microcosm of sorts: art imitating life.

At the south end of our church campus was our Discovery I class, which monthly welcomes newcomers into our church. For a few moments, it became my job to address the forty to fifty fresh faces before me about our church's mission, distinctives, and structure. Most listened attentively, some even jotted down a few notes. But the truth is, most of these newcomers were more concerned about their own personal fates than they were for what I was sharing. Like most newcomers, they could be described as:

- Anxious
- Fearful
- Lonely
- Needy
- Confused
- Protective

After finishing my comments, I left and walked quickly to the opposite end of the campus. There, another meeting—this one for Common Cause community group leaders—was already under way. Here were the experienced bridge builders of our church, opened to love the world, filled with passion and confidence—people who now understand what it means for real purpose to nest in a soul. Each couple or person before me was responsible for leading a small group ministry designed to penetrate the world with God's incarnational love.

Here the environment was charged. The room felt electric. Tonight they were celebrating—celebrating the victories won and the many hours faithfully invested. There were speeches of appreciation, rounds of applause, tears of joy, and even occasional cheers.

God seemed big here. Big. Over the years, personal concerns had somehow given way to ministry concerns. With few exceptions, most of the people around me could be described as:

- Committed
- Courageous
- Connected
- Fruitful
- Focused
- Productive

Two rooms. Two meetings. Two entirely different experiences. Nervous raw recruits on one side. Steady spiritual heroes on the other. It's the church end-to-end—literally, experientially, spiritually. The question is, how does a person go from:

- Anxious to Committed?
- Fearful to Courageous?
- Lonely to Connected?
- Needy to Fruitful?
- Confused to Focused?
- Protective to Productive?

How does a church move its people from one end to the other? What are the primary catalysts for such a dynamic transition? Let me tell you this: It is no easy process.

The distance between those two rooms, although small on an odometer, is only crossed through the slow and often painful process of life integrated with faith and love. You can project this transformation effortlessly on an overhead screen from a church computer or fashion it into a church vision statement. But sanctification, bound in print and tied to theory, is nothing if it does not translate into real life change.

How does a church move its people from personal agendas to kingdom causes?

The movement from one room to another—from preoccupied self-absorption to radical and sacred self-giving—is the movement of faith *in* the real world and *to* the real world. The very places where ministry and life get messy.

REAL OBSTACLES

Church work never occurs on a sterile assembly line. People are not lifeless products rolling passively through a tidy church structure, adjusted spiritually here and tweaked philosophically there. People are people. They are unique personalities teeming with an endless variety of emotional, social, and spiritual makeups. They have wills, needs, agendas, fears, and dreams of their own. To care for them and help them live like Christians is, by itself, a daunting task for any church. But to add to that the challenge of finding ways to transition them into areas of effective service can seem overwhelming, especially when they balk, quite naturally, at the critical ideas of sacrifice, discipline, and giving.

Is it any wonder that churches so often settle for much less than what God has called them to do? If spiritual maturity is defined in terms of living the life *and* serving the world (which it should be), then most evangelical churches are, at best, investing in only the first half of the battle. Today we need the additional investment of developing a process that relentlessly equips people to serve better, not just live better. If not, we doom them to a self-focused immaturity and the church to the sidelines of the community.

> *If spiritual maturity is defined in terms of living the life and serving the world, then most evangelical churches are, at best, investing in only the first half of the battle.*

But people are still people. Just to join a church requires clearing personal hurdles of fear, confusion, and isolation. Every newcomer ventures into the strange land of the church asking, "What are these people here really like? Will I fit in? Will I make friends? Will I be accepted? Will I like it? Will there be a place for me?" These are very real personal obstacles in making the transition to becoming part of a local church community.

Now imagine the personal transition to i²! Making this move usually involves a reversal of critical perspective: from being served to serving, from finding community *in* the church to impacting the community *as* the church, from retreating to influencing, from isolation to engagement, from the church of my needs to the church of good deeds. I would challenge anyone to find a greater or more dramatic personal transition. It's huge!

At Fellowship Bible Church, we have found that there are four primary roadblocks that one must personally overcome in order to transition into and embrace i² ministry. In our setting, these personal obstacles are best dealt with before or during the move from Seasons of Life to Common Cause. If they go unaddressed, our structure may "graduate" a person or a couple into a Common Cause service group, but the personal heartfelt desire necessary for the ministry of irresistible influence simply won't be there. Instead, they will be passive, passionless participants whose bland hearts retard the spiritual influence others are working so hard to release.

In the transition from Seasons of Life to Common Cause, these four personal roadblocks could be charted as follows:

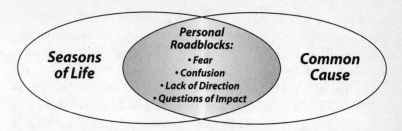

Obstacle #1: Fear

Fear may be the biggest enemy to personal ministry, and a large part of leadership's responsibility will be in helping people move through it.

I recently heard of a small church in Ohio that was contemplating building bridges into its community. Although the Great Commandment is a difficult thing to argue against, one honest member of the church protested. "This is our church," he said, "and we don't want to give it up. It is vitally important to us." With his objection, the man was giving a profound voice to the reality of bridge work: if the church became serious about penetrating the community with God's love, it would be costly—to him, to others he loved, and to their serene and cultivated sense of identity. The resulting traffic would change everything.

The man was right. With i² ministry, change is inevitable and constant, and personal sacrifices are costly. But he was wrong about one critical detail, an incorrect pronoun: the church is never *ours* but always *his*. And he, the God of the Cosmos, wants us to build bridges to the real world. He never intended the church to live the lifestyle of islanders.

Courage, therefore, is the ongoing necessity for i² ministry. American poet Walt Whitman put it this way:

> O we can wait no longer,
> We too take ship, O soul,
> Joyous we launch out on trackless seas,
> Fearless for unknown shores.[1]

This is the spirit of expectation, courage, and high adventure I long for in the people of Fellowship Bible Church as they think about themselves and building bridges to the world around them.

Unfortunately, these are *not* the first emotions our people feel! Not when it comes time for them to think seriously about how they can personally make a difference "out there," beyond the safe borders of our church. No, the predominant emotion is the one that lurks quietly, but all too effectively, behind the shiny exteriors of most evangelicals. It's called *fear*. In my opinion, fear—and not love—is the reality driving most churches. This fear is real, multidimensional, and often paralyzing. It lurks in the shadows and stalks its victims in many forms. First, there is the fear of the unknown—that great, big scary world *out there*, which we see erupting in violence and decadence across our television screens on the nightly news. And God knows, it is an often terrifying world. Yet isolation breeds and multiplies fear, propelling the imagination to envision the world as even more threatening than it really is.

Isolation breeds and multiplies fears, propelling the imagination to envision the world as even more threatening than it really is.

Another all-too-common fear is that of inadequacy. This fear is full of biblical precedent. When God called Moses out to address the squalid conditions of Israel in that oppressive community called Egypt, Moses balked. He balked because of his personal fear of inadequacy:

> The LORD said, "I have indeed seen the misery of my people in Egypt. I have heard them crying out because of their slave drivers, and I am concerned about their suffering. . . . So now, go. I am sending you to Pharaoh to bring my people the Israelites out of Egypt." But Moses said to God, "Who am I, that I should go to Pharaoh and bring the Israelites out of Egypt?" (Exodus 3:7, 10–11)

"Who am I?" is every believer's nemesis when considering the call to i² ministry. It is a fear generated predominately by a sense of unworthiness or what we perceive as our lack of ability or both. Moses, of course, could identify on both counts. His personal track record was soiled with ugly demerits. To his countrymen, did he not carry the smell of Egypt? Was he not compromised? A half-breed? And to the Egyptians, was he not a deserter and a murderer? Clearly, from a human perspective, he was not worthy for this mission. To make matters even worse, he stuttered:

Moses said to the LORD, "O Lord, I have never been eloquent, neither in the past nor since you have spoken to your servant. I am slow of speech and tongue" (Exodus 4:10).

This fear of inadequacy often defeats the faith of evangelicals. It's why we take so easily to withdrawing from the world and our communities. It's why we build church "clubs" and successful "fortresses." It's why we would sooner give money to missionaries than give ourselves to our communities.

We're afraid! We don't think we measure up! The task is too big! Our abilities too small! Our lives too sinful!

> "*Who am I?*" is every believer's nemesis when considering the call to i² ministry.

Reclaiming Our Defining Symbol

Symbols are powerful realities. They define, on both conscious and unconscious levels, how we think, perceive, and finally act.

The church, I believe, has largely abandoned its central defining symbol: the cross. Or perhaps it has exchanged it for something a little less threatening and quite a bit more comfortable. In our Western culture, evangelicals seem to portray Jesus more as clean, safe, and accepting than bloody and driven by the cross. We have forgotten the "self-emptying" example Christ set by his life on earth, and we've raised comfort, satiation, and happiness as central banners of the church. We've huddled together in the misguided belief that we can keep out pain and evil. That we can be safe. That we can live like islanders. Crosses, quite naturally, scare us.

> *We have forgotten the "self-emptying" example Christ set by his life on earth, and we've raised comfort, satiation, and happiness as central banners of the church.*

In order for i² ministry to occur, however, the church must reassert the cross—the tension-riddled paradox that joy and suffering, at least in this world, are somehow interconnected. We must reassert the words of Joseph Rickaby: "The Cross does not abolish suffering, but transforms it, sanctifies it, makes it fruitful, bearable, even joyful, and finally victorious."[2]

We must once again believe the words of Jesus himself: "If you wish to find your life, you must first lose it" (Matthew 10:39). Yet the cross has always been a tough sell. So how does one dispel the paralyzing fear that grips so many believers and convince the church that the abundant life resides only through the mystery of the cross, through losing yourself in love for others?

USE STORIES

One means we've used is through the power of story. Few things are more helpful in clarifying a vision than hearing a success story from one of your peers. In our services and through our monthly church magazine, we constantly expose our body to real-life stories about people who have built bridges into the community.

By "success," I do not mean victories cleansed of hassles, setbacks, or even failure. I mean ordinary people who have conquered their fears, picked up their crosses in service to Jesus, persevered through trials and errors, and in time found meaningful and even strategic use of their gifts and lives. In the following three chapters, I will be sharing a number of these stories with you.

By hearing these stories, people not yet on the launching pad receive a glimpse of what it means to live in the shadow of the cross. Every issue and every question gets answered, not in terms of a preacher's sermon, but in terms of a real person— a person like them. Often, a person they know.

Through the power of story, the mystery and much of the fear of serving and engaging the community is drained away.

Through the power of story, the mystery and much of the fear of serving and engaging the community is drained away. Through story, church members come to understand the great cost of ministry, and even more important, its even greater reward: real, deep joy. The kind of joy Hebrews 12:2 talks about when it states that Christ, "for the joy set before him endured the cross, scorning its shame, and sat down at the right hand of the throne of God."

ENLARGE THE CONCEPT OF MINISTRY

In addition to the power of story, we seek to enlarge the concept of what i² ministry means. In the light and shadow of the symbol of the cross, planted in a real world of dire need, the concept of ministry expands. It's inevitable. With the comfortable borders of the church exploded, the limits for the work of the church are practically endless. The tidy definitions of ministry in an isolated and cramped church— teaching Sunday school, ushering, or serving on a board or commit- tee—become inadequate. What matters now is simple: good works that display the love of Christ.

The truth is finally revealed: *Anything* done in the name of Christ, in the name of love, is ministry. *Anything.* Of course, the more it touches real needs and vital areas, the more influential it will be. But nowhere does the Bible "qualify" good works, and neither should we. Instead, we should celebrate the infinite ways people can "go in Christ's name." We must broaden and enrich the concept of personal ministry; we must bless, affirm, and be willing to release our people into areas that may not directly benefit the church itself.

I remember having an early morning breakfast with an advertising executive. He was fairly new at Fellowship Bible Church and spoke of his frustration: "I'm not a church guy," he said rather emphatically. "I can give money, but I have no interest in ushering. Don't ask me to teach, either. I tried that in my previous church."

"Sounds like you've exhausted all your options," I said with a smile. "So, what do you want to do?"

"What I'm doing right now," he replied. "Contracting and pro- ducing high quality advertising."

"Ever thought of doing that for the church?" I asked.

"You're kidding!" he said.

"No, I'm not!" I countered. "What about helping us speak to the community with thirty-second sermons?"

Two years and several TV commercials later, not only had this "ministry" made an impact on our community (one made front-page headlines), but our church had actually won an advertising award, an "Addy," for its effort.

For too long the church has been trying to turn people into some- thing they are not. And it only fuels their fears of inadequacy. How much better to go with the grain and transform who they *are* into min- istry. Let their passion for public schools, politics, sports, the elderly, city development, moral issues, and yes, even advertising, be potential areas of ministry.

By enlarging the concept of what i2 ministry means, the fear of "Who Am I?" often dissolves, replaced first with something like, "You're kidding," and then with an excitement of possibility and expectation.

PROVIDE FIRST HAND MINISTRY EXPOSURES

A third and final way we address fear is through firsthand ministry exposures. As I said in the previous chapter, the church must provide i2 exposures for its members by programming them into its yearly calendar. In so doing, it gives fearful people a feel for the different kinds of ministry that are "out there," but in a short and safe context. It also gives them a personal experience of their own to go along with the success stories they keep hearing about from other church members.

Fear is one of those "Goliaths" that stalks the church and keeps many from believing they can personally contribute to i2 bridge building. But with the power of story, a broader, more biblical understanding of ministry, and periodic firsthand ministry exposures, this giant can be brought down.

Obstacle #2: Confusion

Having just walked a daughter through college graduation and into the workforce, I know how confusing this life transition can be. Like any graduating senior lost in "What now?" she needed a process. She needed clear tracks that removed some of the mystery, systematized her efforts, and pressed her to a decision. She needed help in selecting personal contacts, choosing job interviews, and making hard decisions.

Every major transition in life needs a process to clear away the fog and create forward momentum.

Every major transition in life needs a process to clear away the fog and create forward momentum. As church members at Fellowship Bible Church approach their graduation from Seasons of Life, "What now?" always raises its ugly head. How do I make sense of all that's about to happen to me? How do I make good decisions? What do I do?

We have a *process*.

Small groups at Fellowship meet from August until June, leaving July for a time of concentrated mission trips, small group leader training, rest, and general preparation for the next year.

For those who are finishing their three-year commitment to a Seasons of Life community group, the formal transition into Common Cause ministry begins the first of April and extends through June. It is a process that gets under way with a "Transition Kickoff" before the entire church. The pastors who lead our Common Cause congregation provide everyone with a handout overview of the steps ahead. This handout offers the following outline:

COMMON CAUSE WORKSHEET

Transition Kickoff (April)

- Pray for God's direction as process begins.
- Get information about Common Cause groups.
- Meet personally with pastors.

Processing (May)

- Visit with existing Common Cause leaders for information about their groups.
- Visit with Common Cause pastors about new group ideas or new group formation.
- Attend the Common Cause Service Fair and talk with service group representatives about ways you can get involved.
- Attend the May "Help Session."
- Continue to pray and follow weekly updates.

Decision Time (June)

- Attend June "Help Session."
- Narrow your options.
- Choose a Common Cause group (new or ongoing) based on your priorities, your gifting, and the interviews you have conducted.
- Contact the group leader and join the group (remember, it is a one-year commitment).

Our process, of course, is being continually refined. For instance, we now ask everyone who is graduating into Common Cause to make sure they have completed a "Servants by Design" seminar before our Spring transition begins. This four-week seminar helps members of our church gain clarity about their gifts and abilities as well as the kinds of ministry settings where they can best be used. In the May and June "Help Sessions," we now offer assistance to church members for interviewing the leaders of prospective Common Cause groups they might be interested in joining. We also offer help for husbands and wives in making a "team decision."

By providing a clearly defined process for people to follow, confusion about the transition to ministry is reduced. Most importantly, the question of "how" has been answered.

Obstacle #3: Lack of Direction

The greater question, though, is not "how?" but "what?" It's not just a matter of "What can I do?" but of "What do I *want* to do? What really *excites* me?" When it comes to serving the kingdom, these are the vital, crucial questions. No one wants to merely put in time. People want purpose, meaning, and fulfillment in their serving. Anything less will feel like Israel's "forced labor" in Egypt: empty, oppressive. And anything less will not propel people through the inevitable pain and difficulty that comes from time to time in having a ministry.

> *No one wants to merely put in time. People want purpose, meaning, and fulfillment in their serving.*

At Fellowship Bible Church, answering the question of direction revolves around two central components: *design* and *ideas*.

Of course, linking one's personal design to specific areas of service is as old as the Bible. Paul, in particular, exhorted the church, not just to good works, but to good works "according to the grace given us" (Romans 12:6 NASB). Every believer has been uniquely endowed and designed by God with different gifts and different abilities, aimed specifically at different functions. Thus, when it comes to serving, what area of ministry would excite one will not necessarily excite another. As Paul clearly states, "And since we have gifts that differ . . .

let each exercise them accordingly" (Romans 12:6, NASB). Each person's God-given gifts and abilities, therefore, become the opening clues to ultimately finding a meaningful and satisfying area of service.

To help people at Fellowship make an even clearer connection between their unique design and an area of service, we created a four-week training seminar called "Servants by Design." This seminar goes beyond the typical spiritual gifts inventory by taking into account not only the idea of spiritual gifts but also one's natural talents and motivations. By coming to a better understanding and appreciation of how God has "wired" each individual overall, one can more fully grasp the range of personal ministry options.

To help people at Fellowship make an even clearer connection between their unique design and an area of service, we created a four-week training seminar called "Servants by Design."

This seminar, built around a "Living by Design" personality test that our church developed in partnership with psychologists Dr. Bob Maris and Dr. Taibi Kahler, helps a person to specifically identify the kinds of things that bring energy and motivation to his or her life: preferences of subject matter, environment, and roles. "Living by Design" is taken before the seminar actually begins so that the results can be examined during the training, thereby wedding the personal information with seminar interaction. People not only come to appreciate that they are "fearfully and wonderfully made" (Psalm 139:14) by their Creator, but they also learn ways to consider their unique design in regard to a particular i² ministry. Information about the "Servants by Design" seminar and the "Living by Design" personality test can be obtained at www.fellowshipassociates.com.

At the start of the seminar, small groups are formed to help each participant personally process the weekly lecture information as well as his or her specific "Living by Design" test. Together, these "dream teams" help each member of the group to brainstorm how their unique gifts and abilities can be creatively connected to ministry "according to the grace given [them]" (Romans 12:6). The sky is the only limit in this "dream team" interaction.

For many, the personal discoveries made during this "Servants by Design" training are nothing less than stunning. Some not only come to see for the first time in what areas they connect with passion, but they are also affirmed by others. "You will be great here," they hear their teammates say. "That so fits you!"

Some even end up doing drastic things—like leaving their jobs! Cheri Faust, for example, had worked for twenty years in retail sales management and merchandising. But something within her felt dissatisfied. She was looking for "meaningful work, work with a purpose." But she didn't know how she could be used in the kingdom of God.

So where is Cheri today? She's the manager of our church bookstore. It's a ministry that fits her perfectly. She says she "can't wait to come in each day."

"Servants by Design" speaks to one side of the "What?" question. Ministry *ideas* speak to the other. As I've already noted, most Christians have a limited understanding of what the church means by "ministry." It's one of the key reasons their gifts often remain unused. That's why ministry ideas are critical. If the church cannot identify, expand, and propagate potential areas of ministry, frustration will build.

At Fellowship Bible Church, ministry ideas flow from a number of spigots. Our existing Common Cause groups are one source. Every year, church members are exposed to the more than eighty groups that have focused causes of involvement. Every year, these groups open to receive new members. They can also identify gifts they desperately need. This in itself offers a rich source of ideas to which one can connect his or her unique design. And many do.

Another source of ideas is from the annual "Service Ministry Fair" that we hold during the transition months of April to June when "Seasons of Life" graduates are contemplating places of service. In addition to exposing the graduates to many of the Common Cause groups at Fellowship, the fair gives representatives from many of the nonprofit agencies around central Arkansas the opportunity to come and present their needs and opportunities.

This last year, I watched in amazement as three hundred of our people crowded into a large auditorium and "shopped" for a ministry with agencies such as the American Red Cross, Arkansas Rice Depot,

Bethany Christian Services, Big Brothers and Big Sisters, Regional AIDS Interfaith Network, Literacy Action of Central Arkansas, United Way, various inner-city ministries, and many others. These ministries set up booths, creatively displaying their objectives and needs. It was an energetic atmosphere, a literal job fair that meshed the church with the community. But more importantly, it generated a host of ministry ideas to members of our church.

Still another source of ministry ideas is the church staff. Each year we create a list of ideas that we believe meet strategic needs both in our church and in the community at large. These ideas have frequently connected with people lacking either motivation or direction. Whether people know it or not, what many lack is simply the creative idea to get them started. They are like potential writers without a thesis.

> *Whether people know it or not, what many lack is simply the creative idea to get them started.*

Yet even with this structured help, many can still feel directionless for a variety of reasons. Even after they know their design and connect with ministry ideas, the reality of serving still needs more personal processing. People are—people. For those still stuck in indecision, Fellowship offers one more directional opportunity: "i² groups."

For one year after Season of Life graduation, members of these "processing" groups meet to consider, dream, and pray together about potential areas of ministry they could, with enthusiasm, commit their personal gifts and abilities to. Overall, we have found these groups to be extremely successful, permitting busy people the time they need to take seriously this issue of service. And if one additional year is needed to help people authentically answer the question of direction, it's worth it!

Obstacle #4: Questions of Impact

While other roadblocks to i² ministry are emotional or pragmatic, this final obstacle is rooted in faith. It comes down to this: Do I really believe in the concept of i² ministry? Do I think it valuable or, still more unsettling, even possible? In other words, should it or can it really be done?

These are usually not screaming doubts but rather uncomfortable whispers of the soul: "It won't do any good. The need is so great, the problems so weighty, the community so corrupt—any effort that is given will at best be only token. So why even do it? Nothing will change!"

Then there's the even more focused pessimism of "What difference can I make? I have very little that I can offer."

While not stated openly, these questions are deeply felt. In my mind, much of our present evangelical apathy is tied to a philosophical surrender of the hope for doing any good. Since the world is hopelessly lost and, for many, the Rapture is our escape, it becomes much easier to critique the world for its evil than to work in it for its good.

Philosophical questions about impact are best answered theologically. Certainly the early church had cause to question their impact both personally and ultimately. What difference could they make? They were, at best, a minuscule group, infinitesimally small in terms of generating any real change. And even if they could make a difference, how could anyone believe that difference would ultimately do any long-term good? After all, we're talking about the Roman Empire, perhaps the most resilient and powerful civilization ever to govern the face of the earth.

Though we stand in awe of what ultimately was accomplished, the truth is that the apostles never proceeded with a view to "success." Not, at least, in the choice of action verbs we choose to define success: *conquer, overcome, win.* Nowhere in Scripture do you find success like this as the objective or the promise. And yet these believers gave themselves relentlessly to the ancient world, which they too knew was passing away (1 John 2:17). They "invaded" it, loved it, served it, and enriched it with their good works.

Why? Two reasons.

First, *they saw themselves entrusted by God with a special calling, a sacred duty to service.* Impact, as we think of it, was not their goal; faithful stewardship was. As the apostle Paul testified in 1 Corinthians 4:1–2, "So then, men ought to regard us as servants of Christ and as those entrusted with the secret things of God. Now it is required that those who have been given a trust must prove faithful."

Second, *they measured success by how much they loved, not by how much the culture changed.* These early Christians no doubt felt "successful," but it was not because they measured it in terms of winning and losing, by numbering evangelical notches on their toga belts. No, to them, the objective in their love and service was bringing glory to God. Whether they were employing their gifts or giving up their lives, success was simply "glorifying the Lord." Peter makes this exact point when he says:

> Each one should use whatever gift he has received to serve others, faithfully administering God's grace in its various forms. If anyone speaks, he should do it as one speaking the very words of God. If anyone serves, he should do it with the strength God provides, so that in all things God may be praised through Jesus Christ. To him be the glory and the power for ever and ever. Amen. (1 Peter 4:10–11)

So, when we say, "What difference can I make?" we frankly pose the wrong question. We should ask, "What stewardship has God called me to render?" Period. This is all that will matter in eternity.

And when we say, "It won't do any good!" we need to be reminded what "good" is. If God has been glorified, we have done good. Real good.

When we say, "It won't do any good!" we need to be reminded what "good" is. If God has been glorified, we have done good. Real good.

It may seem I have made too much of this last roadblock of "What difference will it make?" But I believe that in calling people to build a bridge called i² and then personally participating in it, they must be able to personally address this haunting question of impact. Our life here on earth rests in the answers.

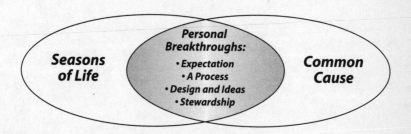

Seasons of Life

Personal Breakthroughs:
• *Expectation*
• *A Process*
• *Design and Ideas*
• *Stewardship*

Common Cause

Fear, confusion, lack of direction, questions of impact. These constitute the nagging realities of the *personal* side of i² ministries. This is where real people live. But through the help of the church, critical breakthroughs can and should occur. Instead of fear, expectation; instead of confusion, a process; instead of a lack of direction, design and ideas; instead of questions of impact, a commitment to stewardship.

This has certainly been the transforming experience of many people at Fellowship Bible Church. Their stories and how they moved from passive spectating and personal agendas to passionate commitment and kingdom causes is next.

And to God, the glory.

BRIDGE BUILDER QUESTIONS

How does your church overcome the personal roadblocks members have of fear, confusion, lack of direction, and questions of impact that so often hold them back from engaging in kingdom causes?

What insight offered in this chapter could be applied to your church right now?

PART THREE

EXPERIENCING THE RESULTS

True Stories of

i² in Action

CHAPTER 6

HOLY SURPRISES

Now to him who is able to do immeasurably

more than all we ask or imagine, according to

his power that is at work within us . . .

—Ephesians 3:20

A BRIDGE STORY

A great bridge—either real or metaphoric—is always a work of art. And as a work of art, a good share of a bridge's greatness depends on the uniqueness of its engineer: his or her experience, passion, gifts, temperament, personality, and perspective. In our own country, for example, the great bridges are but long shadows of their builders: the majestic and sturdy Brooklyn Bridge birthed from the tenacious genius of the Roeblings, father and son; the graceful Golden Gate from the pint-sized Joseph Strauss; the simple and elegant lines of the Hudson River Bridge from the artistic Othmar Ammann. These are just three of many examples. Great bridges, in a deep fashion, are the creations of their engineers.

But never theirs alone.

In Engineers of Dreams, *author Henry Petroski writes of the essentially communal and integrated nature of bridge building:*

Engineers can dream alone, but they can seldom bring their dreams to fruition by solitary effort. The roots of large-project engineering, such as bridge building, lie in military operations, which necessarily involve generals and soldiers, chieftains and Indians. Though the chief engineer may be the one who holds the grand plan in his head, it may ever remain his dream alone unless he can command a staff of engineers to direct still others to commit the concept to paper, to carry out the voluminous calculations that flesh out the dream and put a price on it, and to make the numerous drawings of details that allow it all to come together in the field.[1]

A great bridge is always the work of the diversified many, a creation as wonderful as each one of its many individual creators.

I CALL THEM "HOLY UNEXPECTEDS." You labor obediently and some-times courageously to follow God's will, and then, unexpectedly, he makes it more than you could ever imagine.

"Holy unexpecteds." Of all the surprises in life, the most satisfy-ing are when you become aware that God is actively involved—blessing, empowering, supernaturally advancing even your best efforts beyond your highest dreams.

I trust you've had moments like these. They bring a special joy, a divine affirmation, a sense of the eternal. You realize that you have stepped on holy ground and have become a partner in the process of passing on everlasting life. Nothing gives the heart a transcendent leap like this.

For several years I have possessed a quiet confidence in my heart that our church was not only headed in the right direction, but that our i² commitment of bridge building also was being favored by God. Turn-ing the face of the church outward, giving its resources away, blessing the community, unleashing the gifts of laypeople to serve—this is what our living God desires for his church in complementing and balancing its effort of proclaiming the Good News. It has been hard work, but it has also become clear that we are not alone. Added to all we've done have been these wonderful, sacred moments that shout, *"Surprise! God is here!"* It becomes evident that God wants this to succeed more than we ever imagined! You sense him telling you, "Your faith is being rewarded. Keep going!"

One of these surprises occurred recently when a representative from Harvard University called to request permission to do a case study on our church. "Why?" I asked with an initial sense of disbelief. "What on earth would pair Fellow-ship Bible Church with Harvard?"

The caller went on to explain that the John F. Kennedy School of Government at Harvard was working with FaithWorks, a branch of Bob Buford's fine organization, Leadership Network, to host a national conference on social entrepre-neurship. He was helping write case studies that would give conference participants some living

Turning the face of the church outward, giving its resources away, blessing the community, unleashing the gifts of laypeople to serve—this is what our living God desires for his church.

examples of effective social engagement with community life. Fellowship Bible Church had been selected to be one of the six case studies presented. In fact, it was to be the "only church in the mix," the caller said. "Because you are known for helping laypeople cross over into the needs of the community, we felt it was important that your story be told."

Harvard University and Fellowship Bible Church. For a moment, I felt like Sarah laughing incredulously behind her tent. But a moment of divine favor is no laughing matter. It is, on the contrary, one more holy surprise to be enjoyed and savored.

Yet not even a call from Harvard could equal the real-life surprises we have regularly received from our own people here at Fellowship. Certainly, we have worked and prayed for years to move them with their gifts into various forms of ministry engagement within our community. But quite frankly, no one in our church at the beginning would have dared imagine how creative and effective some of our people and their small groups would ultimately be. As I look back to when the idea of mobilizing people into Common Cause groups for the purpose of i² service first began, I must confess that neither I nor anyone else in leadership would have believed what, in fact, is happening now.

> *I must confess that neither I nor anyone else in leadership would have believed what, in fact, is happening now.*

In this chapter and the two that follow, I want to share a few of the stories of the "diversified many" who have been faithful bridge builders in our own church—people who have often faced real fears, deep feelings of inadequacy, problems, and difficulties—and yet, because of courage and persistence, have run unexpectedly into success.

JIM AND CONNIE PHILLIPS: MOVING OFF THE SIDELINES

Jim Phillips was watching a basketball game when it hit him. "The game was between two Christian high school teams, and I found myself thinking, 'My faith is a spectator sport; I watch it more than I live it.'" Jim's life was full of good things, but he felt restless. Life had become a wash of "sameness": common routines, learned patterns, repetitious structure. He was making a good living as a successful CPA, had a wonderful family, and was involved in our church. But he sensed he lacked the most important thing: *life-giving passion.*

He went home and told his wife, Connie, what he was thinking. He felt it was time to step off the sidelines and into the painful reality of the world. They would have to do something *intentional.* But what? After much soul-searching, this is what they felt God was leading them to do: they would pull their kids from Christian schools and enroll them in a public school system that was struggling under mounting problems. Then they would get involved as parents in that school and look for opportunities to serve.

Although they would choose the best possible public school for their children, they knew they were gambling on faith. Both of them knew that their lives would never be the same. Moving the family out of its carefully crafted comfort zone would invite feelings of loneliness, fear, isolation, and hurt.

When Connie went to pick up her four children after their first day of public school, she got her first taste of their family's new reality. She found them huddled together and alone on a bench in front of the school. They were beginning to understand the cost of their parents' decision to reach the world with God's love and the cross you must sometimes bear. The Phillips's journey of courageous faith had begun.

Eventually they found themselves paired with Larry and Ann McGraw. Because of each couple's growing public school experience, they saw the need not only for mentoring but also for sexual abstinence teaching. So together they formed a Common Cause group at Fellowship Bible Church with this ministry in mind. In time they developed and taught a sexual abstinence and mentoring program called Excel, a program that they have now used in nearly all the public junior high schools in their district. Through the efforts of their Common Cause group, they recently received federal funding that allowed them to hire a program director and two part-time employees.

Today they are welcomed with open arms by thirteen different public schools in Pulaski County. More than 3,500 students are now involved with Excel as well as 700 adult volunteers. "One of the most exciting things has been seeing God raise up sixty-five local churches, in addition to Fellowship, that have stepped in and contributed time and resources for their particular area schools," Connie says. "That's a key to success."

Last year the Excel staff even presented their program in the Cayman Islands in the Western Caribbean. And in Little Rock they are now starting "Class Act" clubs in some of the schools as an opportunity to follow up the weeklong abstinence programs.

Jim and Connie Phillips are no longer in the stands with a spectator kind of faith. They are fully deployed with a faith that not only has broken a sweat but is filled with the life-giving passion Jim once dreamed about.

DAVE KELLA: A WAY TO THE HEART OF THE INNER CITY

Two years after moving to Little Rock with his promotion to lead IBM-Arkansas, Dave Kella became chairman of strategic planning for the Pulaski County United Way fund drive. As he came to understand the deep needs of Little Rock's inner city, he began wondering if enough funds or enough programs would ever be available to make a real impact.

Dave and five other men from our church began to investigate ways in which they could connect the needs of the poor with the enormous resources common to the people in their world. In 1995 they attended a luncheon at a private Christian school in one of the worst parts of the inner city. To a man, they were impressed with the hope, manners, and hunger to learn that they observed in these often overlooked and neglected children.

"I saw these kids who were well-disciplined and smiling," Dave recalls. "One second grader came up, looked me in the eye, shook my hand, and said with a smile, 'My name's Timothy.' They were so glad to meet us. The conclusion I reached was, if we change the heart of the inner city, we'll change the inner city." As important as all the funding and programs were, the key was changing people.

This group of six soon became a board, unleashing their natural bent toward creativity, management, and driving connections. In gifts, skills, temperament, and passion, they flourished in doing the work of the kingdom.

Once crippled by poor infrastructure and an inability to fund teachers and parent tuition discounts, that same Little Rock inner-city

Christian school is now blossoming with an enrollment of over 1000. Much of that progress is due to the partnership Dave and the rest of the board members have provided. Some of these students have even been mentored, one on one, by these men.

Last year the board—now known as the Christian Educational Assistance Foundation—doubled in size, hired a full-time executive director, and expanded its vision and operations. This year, by recruiting donors to fund private vouchers, CEAF, working in tandem with a national scholarship organization, will give away more than 1,500 educational scholarships to poor children not only locally but throughout the state of Arkansas in both religious and secular schools.

For Dave, it shows what Jesus Christ can do when brothers dwell together in unity.

MARY ANN TURNER: FINDING HER OWN MINISTRY

At first Mary Ann Turner felt she just didn't fit. Her husband, John, wanted to participate in a Common Cause group for Habitat for Humanity, a ministry that involves laypeople in building homes for needy families. But she didn't know an eight-penny nail from a hole in the ground. What good could she do? And to be honest, she wasn't excited about going into the inner city of Little Rock, where most of the Habitat homes were built. She knew what these neighborhoods were like. This was asking for some kind of crazy trouble.

But a quote from one of our pastors stuck in her mind: "If you want to be out where God is, you have to take your eyes off your surroundings." So she did. Mary Ann began meeting and interacting with the residents of the Habitat homes, talking about recipes and babies and approaching weather fronts. Soon she was taking her children with her.

She and John quickly noticed that some of the Habitat families were letting their homes fall into decay after moving in. They had always been tenants, and they didn't fully understand the responsibilities of owning a home. They didn't know who to call if they had a problem or how to make repairs.

Along with another couple, John and Mary Ann decided to begin their own Habitat Common Cause group with a different focus: helping a family maintain their Habitat home once it was built.

The first year was the hardest. They called families, some of whom had been in Habitat homes for more than a decade. But even friendly invitations, from a voice that sounded "white" over the phone, were viewed with suspicion. They spent large amounts of time building relationships one by one. "At first the response to us was, 'Who is this white group coming in here?'" Mary Ann says. "It took some time to develop trust."

Using relational skills that come naturally to her, Mary Ann started meeting with some of the residents socially. She offered tips. She served up herself as a bridge to social service agencies and community services. She hooked up with other Common Cause groups, who offered help with things like budgets and mentoring.

The second year, with trust now established, she helped a number of Habitat residents form a homeowner's association.

Now when she reads of gang violence, Mary Ann doesn't turn the page; she checks to see how close it was to her friends. Love has made the difference. It has also made an impact. Habitat for Humanity was so impressed with the work of Mary Ann's Common Cause group that they have adopted it locally, forming the "Family Nurture Committee."

LARRY AND SONYA MENDELSOHN: REACHING OUT TO INNER-CITY KIDS

Larry and Sonya Mendelsohn have always made a good team. Whether at work or at play, they enjoy operating as a twosome. As they grew in their faith, they naturally began to desire a way to be involved in ministry together.

When the church challenged them to join a Common Cause group and look for a ministry in the community, they wondered if it might be possible to reach out in the inner city of Little Rock. It was an area as far away from their comfortable, suburban neighborhood in the plush and rolling green of West Little Rock as Pluto is from Mercury. They shared the same sun, but that was about it. How is it possible to cross such a distance?

At lunch one day Larry, who leads an oncology-hematology practice in Little Rock, said to me, "We'd like to help the inner city."

I remember telling him, "You might want to narrow that down a bit. Try for a tighter focus. Do just one thing." I also added, "Try coming along with someone who is already working there."

Larry took my advice. In time, he and Sonya settled on helping an already-established social service ministry in an inner-city neighborhood.

The timing was perfect. The ministry there was struggling, needing help and helpers. The next step was logical: "What can we do?"

Together Larry and Sonya put together a Common Cause group that, at first, planned events for the inner-city kids such as retreats, Christmas parties, and other functions. Then came the idea to send these kids to a summer camp that would give them exposure to life outside the harsh realities of their inner-city environment.

That year they held car washes, with the community group and the kids working together to raise money. With the money they made, they sent twenty young people to summer camp. Everyone was thrilled to see the impact the camp had. "Many gang members were saved, and lives changed," Larry said.

But it didn't stop there. The ambitions and the success of the group expanded. They conducted a five-kilometer road race in Little Rock to send even more kids to camp. The first year of the race, they began planning only six weeks out. They didn't have a place, a name, or a sponsor. But people all over the city got involved. A local radio personality donated his time. Corporations gave money. A black choir sang by the river. It worked!

With the proceeds, forty young people were able to go to camp. In addition, $22,000 was left over, part of which was put into an account for special needs and the remainder used to start an inner-city educational scholarship fund. That year twelve inner-city kids got to attend either the Christian high school or college of their choice. One of those students was Don Butler, an outstanding drama student who, without such help, would have been forced to drop out of college. "It's stories like that," Sonya said, "that make it all worthwhile."

Last year the race generated more than $60,000 and made the front page of the newspaper. From those proceeds, Larry and Sonya's Common Cause group sent fifty-five kids to camp and gave out more than $30,000 in scholarship money. "It just keeps growing!" Sonya said. And this year they expect to do even better!

JIM DAVIS: LEAVING A LEGACY

The name of Jim Davis will never make a headline. In fact, it's not his real name. He prefers his kingdom work to remain anonymous.

As CEO of a successful company, Jim had accumulated substantial assets and was approaching his retirement. Spiritually sensitive, he began wrestling with the questions: What will I do with my estate? How should it be used? Where should it be invested? Within a group of his friends, also Christian businessmen, a wide variety of opinions surfaced. He understood that stewardship was not just a question of the here and now but of where your heart resides in eternity. The issue of legacy.

Here is what Jim finally did. After taking care of family matters, he and his wife established a sizable foundation under the direction of the church. It was agreed that any projects funded by foundation money would fit with the vision and purposes of the church. Much of it would be used as seed money to help "jump-start" strategic ministry ventures beyond the reach of Fellowship Bible Church. In other words, this money was not to be used by our church *for* our church, but rather to help advance *other* causes. The foundation board also agreed that it would put special emphasis on aiding the development of new leadership within the church at large.

It was at this same time that Fellowship's staff was dreaming of establishing a company to help train church leaders and plant i2 churches. It was a holy surprise when this new foundation offered seed money for setting up this company by providing funding for its first five years of operation. "Fellowship Associates," as the company came to be called, is today training "blue chip" seminary graduates in a one-year leadership residency program as well as helping plant new churches across the United States.

Meanwhile, Jim's foundation just keeps on giving and giving.

BECKY BRUNS: DISCOVERING GOD'S DESIGN

Becky Bruns remembers a particular Sunday in 1984 when I was preaching about the need for Christians to take a stand against abortion. "I hadn't really thought about this issue," she says, "but I was stirred to get involved." Soon after, with the help of our church, Bethany Christian Services was established in central Arkansas to offer mothers the option of giving up children they are unable to care for to adoption.

Becky and her husband, David, decided to become foster parents for a biracial baby boy. "Taking that foster child gave me a heart for birth mothers," Becky says. "We had that little boy for six weeks, and when he left, our hearts were broken."

Becky also realized that through Bethany, she had the opportunity to combine her college training—a degree in social work—with her passion. "Gifts, passion, and ministry are something continually stressed at Fellowship," she said. She began contract work, assessing adoptive families, and for the last six years has worked full-time for Bethany as a counselor to birth mothers.

Becky was surprised to learn that in our culture, adoption is not always a popular decision. "It's so difficult to give up your child," she said. Still there is no denying the joy and satisfaction Becky experiences each time a loving home is matched with "one of her babies." Adoption is a hard but beautiful choice.

Becky now counsels mothers throughout the state of Arkansas and has also helped disseminate information about adoption into the public schools. In 1997 she was named the International Employee of the Year for Bethany Christian Services.

BILL SMITH: FILLING THE EMPTINESS

Our affluent society in America has produced many wealthy people who are empty inside. They have achieved wealth and status, and they realize there must be something more to life—thus, today's great interest in "spirituality."

This was Bill Smith's experience. A successful financial advisor, he couldn't shake his own sense of emptiness. He tried New Age religion and eastern mysticism among other things, but nothing stuck.

But his life did change during a trip to Salt Lake City. In his hotel room Bill opened a Gideon's Bible and read John 1:12–13: "Yet to all who received him, to those who believed in his name, he gave the right to become children of God—children born not of natural descent, nor of human decision or a husband's will, but born of God." That passage ignited a fire in Bill that has never gone out.

A few years ago I needed someone to serve with me and to act as host for our "Men's Fraternity" meetings. Men's Fraternity is a weekly outreach to men in our community that consistently draws 400 to 500 men to an early morning meeting. Bill was surprised at my challenge, but he took it because he saw that it might give him more opportunities to influence the lives of other men. And it did. Friends and strangers began calling him up, asking for appointments to talk about how they could fill the emptiness in their lives—the same emptiness Christ had filled years before in his heart.

One man who contacted Bill was thinking of taking his life. He was divorced and his ex-wife wouldn't talk to him, he was estranged from his children, and his business was falling apart. "He was in a world of hurt. I had been in some of those fixes myself, so I could certainly identify with some of the feelings he had."

Bill began taking him through "One to One," a Bible study I wrote that helps nonbelievers understand the gospel and confront their need for Christ. Wonderfully, the man received Christ and saw an immediate change in his life. He somehow persuaded his wife to begin attending Fellowship with him, and she received Christ as well. "They are now remarried, his business has turned around, and now he's being used in other's men's lives," Bill says. "He's a tremendous witness."

Bill just turned sixty. His desire to mentor young men—helping them learn how to put God at the center of their lives—is stronger than ever. He regularly consults with churches around the country who want to start a Men's Fraternity in their own communities. He and some friends have even begun a new ministry called "Sportsmen's Quest," in which they take sons of single mothers on hunting and fishing trips. It gives these boys much-needed exposure to the influence of Christian men.

To Bill, the opportunity to influence other men has been a "life giver." He says the last seven years have been the best of his life. "I think there is something about having gray hair," he says with a smile. "Younger men are looking for older men to guide them. I want to keep making myself available."

And in Little Rock today, there are scores of young men who are more than just a little glad Bill does.

CLIFF AND EDIE PARNELL: OVERCOMING FEELINGS OF INADEQUACY

At the age of twenty-seven, Edie met a man she thought would be her partner for the rest of her life. He was a funny man, a man who could make you feel good in almost any situation: bright, personable, gregarious—and also a man with secret passions for alcohol and gambling.

She watched him once make a $500 bet that the University of Arkansas football team would make a touchdown on the next play. She was horrified when he offered her as a sex partner, like she was a generous tip at a restaurant, to a man who had been simply kind enough to drive his drunken body home. Seeking help once, she was told by a pastor that she had to submit, *no matter what,* to what her husband said. She took Valium for courage.

In some ways the divorce ended things—the abuse, the insanity, the nightmare. Yet in other ways, mysterious and confusing, she would spend years in dealing with the ongoing consequences of a broken marriage. She wondered if she could ever accomplish anything good in her life.

Edie eventually married Cliff Parnell, a doctor who was also divorced with two sons. They soon discovered that a new marriage wouldn't solve their problems, but at that point God stepped in and drew them to himself. Cliff and Edie received Christ and began attending our church. Soon grace and forgiveness began to gradually replace their woundedness. And as it did, a new life began to emerge.

Because of their experience with divorce, they felt a special desire to reach out to those who appeared close to marital breakup. But like many of those who have experienced divorce firsthand, they felt a deep sense of inadequacy. "We prayed a lot, asking God, 'Why is divorce becoming so prevalent in the lives around us?'" Cliff says. "But other than the fact that we'd both done it and had a passion to help others *not* do it, we didn't feel equipped to really get involved. Even with the church prodding us to pursue our passion, it was hard."

Still, by faith, they decided to join several other divorced couples in a Common Cause group to help prevent others from ending their marriages needlessly without thought or hope.

As all the couples in the group so painfully knew, a divorce leads to long-term consequences that go on and on: struggles with finances, trust, self-esteem, children, former spouses—you name it. On a retreat, they shared their stories. "The bonding that occurred that weekend was the most incredible thing I have ever experienced," Cliff says.

The group members wrote out their experiences with divorce and put them together in a book that they now give to those considering divorce. Then they meet with couples who, for whatever reason, are looking for a way out of their marriages. Says Edie, "We want to be able to say to a couple in trouble, 'Stop. Don't take any action. Give us five weeks to walk you through this momentous decision you're considering.'"

The unfortunate reality is that a number of the marriages they touch are in such trouble that they do not survive. But each marriage they do save fills Cliff and Edie and the others in their group with hope and encouragement. For Cliff and Edie, the holy surprise is this: God works through less-than-perfect humans.

JIM STRAWN: BECOMING A "LIFE COACH"

Jim Strawn knew he had found a different type of church when he began attending Fellowship in 1981. At the time we were conducting our worship services in the only building we could find—a high school gymnasium with no air-conditioning. On this particular Sunday in August, Jim was driving to church and noticed that the temperature at 10 A.M. had hit 100 degrees. If it was that hot outside, how would it feel in that gym? "There won't be anybody there," he thought.

To his surprise he saw five hundred people jammed into the gym. "I thought, 'Well, maybe these are all religious wackos,'" Jim recalls. "But I looked in and saw bankers and lawyers I knew from the community, and they all looked like intelligent people to me. So I thought, 'There must be something going on here that I need to get plugged into more deeply.'"

Jim was a successful man in the world of business, but he was divorced and felt deep guilt over how he had failed his four children. "What use could I be to anyone, especially to God?" he wondered.

But then Jim came face-to-face with Jesus Christ. "My redemption really did give me a new beginning," he says. And in the years that followed, the church as well as Jim's small group experiences offered him more and more opportunities to connect his faith with a world of need.

One Sunday at church an appeal was made by the director of the STEP ministry (an inner-city ministry begun by our church) for volunteers to serve as mentors in a public elementary school. Each mentor would spend an hour a week helping two children with their schoolwork. "I don't know why—it must have just been the gentle nudging of the Holy Spirit—but I thought, 'I need to do that.'"

He started working with Richard, a third grader. For the first few meetings it didn't seem like Richard was getting anything out of the interaction. After a few meetings more, Jim asked the administrator of the program whether this was worthwhile, and she said, "Oh, he loves it! He just doesn't know how to show it."

The more Jim spent time with Richard, the more he discerned how he could help this little boy. He saw that Richard needed help with his reading and comprehension skills, and he began working with him in these areas. A school counselor suggested that Richard attend an alternative school where he would live five days a week at a camp just outside town. His mother couldn't pick him up on Fridays, so Jim did. Jim told Richard's mother, "I don't want to interfere and insert myself in situations that you don't feel are appropriate. I'm not trying to be his parent, just his friend." She was most appreciative.

As their relationship grew stronger and as years went by, Jim had the opportunity to talk with Richard about all kinds of issues—how to deal with girls, how to deal with jealousy from friends because of his athletic ability, and how to handle—well, *life.* Jim has found that mentoring relationships require becoming a "life coach."

Another relationship he began was with Antwon, who was involved in gangs, had tried to commit suicide, and had dropped out of school after ninth grade. "What that young man needed as much as anything was simply somebody he could talk to and figure out life with," Jim says. "There was no one to guide him in how to do things—how to manage himself, how to get up on time in the morning, how to have polite table manners."

Today Richard is "on track" in high school, actively involved in sports and ROTC. And Antwon, the former high school dropout, eventually returned to school and is now a sophomore at the University of Arkansas. Jim too has come a long way. Best of all, he no longer has questions about his usefulness to God.

MIKE ROBINSON: ENTERING THE "FINAL FRONTIER"

For three decades Mike Robinson had built a successful career as an accountant and financial consultant. He moved up the career ladder and became a senior partner of a ninety-member accounting firm that earns millions in fees annually from across the world.

Last year, he gave all that up to come work at our church.

Mike, who has been an elder at Fellowship for the past fourteen years, has recently assumed the title of Stewardship Director. And, yes, that position involves how people spend and use their money, a subject Jesus addressed almost as much as prayer.

Mike walks a little taller these days. He is convinced that, no matter how much worldly success he once achieved, it pales in comparison to what can happen during the next few years. With fire in his eyes, Mike says emphatically, "Nothing comes close to the satisfaction I receive serving God's kingdom and seeing the wonders the Lord is doing in his church through people. Nothing."

As he consulted with different members of our church over the years, God placed on his heart a special desire. As he explains, "The Lord burdened me with two callings: to help people discover and understand the blessings of biblical stewardship, and to help replace the cultural consumer mindset that infiltrates the church with a restored vision of kingdom work."

Mike feels that biblical stewardship is the "final frontier" of spiritual life. "Too often people view stewardship as their financial obligation to the Lord. I think that's extremely shortsighted," Mike said. "Real stewardship benefits more than it obligates. It transforms us in ways that go far beyond our money. It's what the Lord does *in us* that's so thrilling."

As Stewardship Director, Mike conducts seminars on stewardship, assists in the wise and strategic development of new foundations to help fund i^2 ministry, and provides consulting assistance to church members as well as various ministry leadership boards connected to the church both locally and around the world.

Some of his former associates think that Mike will eventually come to his senses and return to his former job, but Mike thinks otherwise. "As my generation reaches retirement age," he says, "more people of the baby boomer generation will want to be involved in a form of creative giving." And as Mike sees it, he is strategically placed for maximum impact.

ONLY A BEGINNING

God has been good to the people of Fellowship Bible Church. Our people have discovered a cause bigger than fear, bigger than comfort, bigger than wealth, and bigger than any image of success. It has given them life just as Jesus promised. But that's not what has surprised me the most.

When we first began to infuse our church with the vision of i², we knew people would branch out into the community to spread the love of Christ. What we didn't expect was how effective and how creative their ministries would become: that they would write books and organize road races; that they would leave their jobs and go into full-time ministry work, here in Little Rock and even overseas; that they would create their own companies and ministries; that they would establish charitable foundations; that some would even hire their own staff!

When we first began to infuse our church with the vision of i², we knew people would branch out into the community to spread the love of Christ. What we didn't expect was how effective and how creative their ministries would become.

These are the holy surprises. This is also what being an i² church is all about. And yet something tells me we've only seen the beginning.

BRIDGE BUILDER QUESTIONS

What dreams do stories like these stir up in you?

What dreams do they stir up for your church?

CHAPTER 7

WOUNDED HEALERS

*Not that we are competent in ourselves
to claim anything for ourselves,
but our competence comes from God.*

—2 Corinthians 3:5

A BRIDGE STORY

The bridge metaphor or image extends to nearly every major human institution: politics, religion, family, and nation. For example, Bill Clinton once claimed his policies to be a bridge to the new millennium.

The church has seen the bridge as a metaphor or transition from heaven to earth. In medieval times, for example, monks were enjoined to build bridges and streets and thus prepare one's way to heaven.

The Bridges of Madison County, lovely and covered, evoke the nostalgia of romance.

In Ernest Hemingway's For Whom the Bell Tolls, *the bridge in danger, about to be blown up in an act of war, is a shattering symbol of civil war, of the essential human split.*

Part of the versatility of the bridge as a metaphor is its chameleon-like ability to evoke feelings of danger, romance, or nostalgia—sometimes at the same time.

In movies, bridges can establish a tone, a location, even a way of life with a single opening scene. Think of the movies you have seen featuring San Francisco or New York, which did not use the Golden Gate or Brooklyn bridges?

Although diverse, the bridge as metaphor shares a common theme: human connection. And any bridge, either real or imagined, is useless unless one person moves toward another person.

MORE THAN TEN YEARS AGO, Chuck and Susan Taylor came to Fellowship Bible Church looking for life preservers.

In their disconnected lives, they were drowning in a river of pain. From time to time, they surfaced for air, not even capable of understanding the mechanics necessary for building bridges to others. Survival was the only thing on their minds.

"LET ME FIGHT FOR YOU"

Chuck carried with him a legacy of pain. The son of an abusive, alcoholic father, he watched his own dad—in between months-long stays in the hospital—engage in "Friday Nights at the Fights" with his mother, a woman without a high school diploma who believed she had no choice but to surrender to violence. Because his father's chronic illness kept him from working, Chuck got a full-time job when he was eleven.

When Chuck was sixteen, his dad died. For most of his childhood, he was an adult; and for most of his adult life, he was a child. He pursued cheap, quick thrills outside of his marriage. In 1987 his wife asked him for a divorce and said she wanted custody of their four children.

A co-worker, whom Chuck publicly ridiculed as "weak," kept inviting him to Fellowship Bible Church. The invitations continued even after the man became sick with ulcers and had to leave his job. He called again after receiving news that Chuck's wife had left him. And again, Chuck turned him down.

A few weeks later, after Chuck had been hospitalized for symptoms of a heart attack, the man called again. This time Chuck was more receptive; and even though his problem turned out to be only his gall bladder, the hospital visit shook him up.

When Chuck walked into Fellowship, he began eyeing a nice seat somewhere near the aisle, the closer to the exit the better. His friend, however, dragged him to the front row. The message that morning "just happened" to be on the effects of divorce and the long-standing pain it unleashes. Chuck could relate. That day, just a few feet from the pulpit, he began weeping like a baby; the word of God had stirred up a deep pool of grief and regret.

Chuck joined a community group and began to grow in his faith. He convinced himself that God was going to repair his marriage before the divorce became final and keep him from losing custody of his two boys. But as time went on, he began to realize that this wasn't going to happen.

The week before the divorce became final, it was Chuck's turn to bring the drinks to his community group meeting. He called Dennis, the group's leader, and told him he wouldn't be there. When Dennis asked why, Chuck said that Christianity wasn't working for him.

Dennis found out where Chuck was living—in a corner-of-the-attic apartment that smelled like mildew and pizza leftovers. On Super Bowl Sunday, during the game, he came to talk to Chuck. For an hour and a half, Chuck repeated his claim: his faith wasn't working. Dennis told him not to give up. Chuck said, "Thanks, but no thanks." Dennis said, "Let me fight for you."

The next week, Chuck showed up for his community group with his faith mysteriously changed. "What I realized later," Chuck says, "is that it wasn't Dennis saying, 'Let me fight for you,' it was Jesus saying, 'Let me fight for you.'" For Chuck, that moment was a turning point.

AN UNBEARABLE ANGER

Susan too had been devastated by a hurtful marriage. For nine years her former husband had told her she was a bad wife, a bad mother, and a bad person. She had swallowed those words so many times that even after the divorce she could not help but feel the coiled spring of anger from the pit of her stomach. That anger occupied her, often reducing her to a roiling silence. She says she took it out on her two sons.

Her husband's adultery was the last straw.

Soon after she began coming to Fellowship Bible Church as a single mother, a community group began reaching out to her. It was a collection of mostly single, previously divorced people, who helped each other fill in the "voids and lonely hours."

With rusted mufflers hanging onto rusted cars with rusty baling wire, the people in that community group ensured her survival. Women invited her over to cross-stitch. There were movies on Saturdays, potlucks on birthdays, basketball games with her children, a call on an anniversary date she no longer celebrated. For Susan, these were bridges to sanity and survival. Despite the poverty and endless chaos that is the life of many single parents, these were, in some unexpected ways, some of the good times.

But the anger never went away. With life, with herself, with others, with God.

Yet often when she felt her anger becoming unbearable, someone would surprise her with a show of special love. One time she shared with the church that she could not find any strong male role models for her two sons; even most of the coaches her boys played for were females. Three families started including her children in some of their family activities. For the first time, she really understood the theology of the grace of God and the church as extended family.

Still the lonely hours could not all be filled. There were deep dives into guilt and anger. She always felt so vulnerable, so fragile. Even with frequent glimpses of grace, her faith was constantly being challenged by the hard reality of life.

A DEEPENING FRIENDSHIP

In the lives of both Chuck and Susan, God was doing a slow, painful, and powerful work.

To find hope in their future, strength for their present, and for-giveness for their pasts, Chuck and Susan learned to cling to faith like a man clings to a ripcord on his first parachute jump. The trust of the white-knuckled. They both made seemingly impossible commitments to move forward. The vision and teaching of the church, fleshed out in the love of their community groups, was the catalyst for change. Quite simply, they could not have made it without the support of the church.

Susan, in addition to her responsibilities as a single parent, made a vow to "know who she was and know who she could be." She signed up for classes in church. Once again, she began to get a new vision for her life, a life embedded in the potential of church. Susan says the com-mitment to change was deep: "I felt like I had wasted a lot of my life, but that I had not wasted it all. If I would let God work on me, I could change." Hope was the anchor when she seemed weightless with despair.

When Chuck and Susan finally met one another, they had no desire for anything other than friendship. Romantic love had betrayed them both. So when Chuck volunteered to come over and play basketball with her boys, Susan was direct: "If you are looking for anything other than friendship, you can hit the road now." Chuck felt relieved. Neither held terribly high opinions about the possibilities of marriage. And so the friendship blossomed.

Then Chuck received a surprising phone call from one of his sons. "Dad, are you coming home today? Mom is gone." His former wife had begun to unravel after their divorce and had abandoned the four children. When he arrived at his former home, he found it in terrible disarray and decay; the smell was nearly overpowering.

Chuck had become a single father. It was what he wanted, but soon overwhelming questions were exploding around him: How do you get the kids up every morning and ready for school? How do you take care of them when they are sick and you still have to go to work? How do you shop for groceries and clean the house and do the laundry and keep up with homework and take them to the zoo? And sleep? And find time to lick your own wounds? He felt like he needed to schedule an appointment to take a breath.

His friendship with Susan began to run deep. In mutual desperation and compassion they helped one another. They encouraged one another. They fought for one another. Then one day they realized there was more to their relationship than friendship. They got married. Then, in their words, "all hell broke loose."

"THE BRADY BUNCH FROM HELL"

"Blended families" could rank as one of contemporary culture's greatest oxymorons. The *Brady Bunch* should be outlawed on the grounds that it tells more lies than a tobacco official being questioned by a Senate subcommittee. "We had these four boys—all of them under the age of fourteen—who wouldn't naturally choose each other as friends, and we threw them together and asked them to call it a family," says Chuck. "We were the Brady Bunch all right. The Brady Bunch from hell."

In fact, Chuck and Susan had little good to bring to their second marriage, a history of poor self-esteem, previous marriages ended by abuse or breakdown. Still, knowing the length of the odds, Chuck and

Susan made a commitment up front: divorce was *not* an option. "We knew what divorce does," Susan says, "and we made a vow never to do it again. We could kill each other, but not divorce."

That vow, they both say now, is the only thing that kept them together. Power struggles were immediate and overwhelming. Chuck, for example, could not tolerate Susan's oldest boy sitting at the breakfast table, holding out an empty glass, and tersely saying, "Milk," and Susan jumping up and filling it. One of Chuck's daughters would sometimes come home from college just long enough to cause a scene and tell her father that she "hated him."

Chuck and Susan understood the riptides of underlying issues. But they found themselves in a catch-22: the chaos of the present was mostly caused by issues from the past, but the chaos of the present demanded almost all of their time and energy. "Hate" is not too strong a word to use about how all of the family members felt, at one point or another, about each other.

Unlike many comfortable middle-class, middle-aged Christians, Chuck and Susan have rarely questioned the necessity of God in their lives. Without him, they would both probably be dead by now or in some condition very near to it. In both of their lives, circumstances have forged hearts of dependence on God. The vow to stay married forced them to look for creative solutions.

THE PARADOX OF SERVING OTHERS

Once again the church proved to be a lifesaver. They both received extensive counseling, took classes on such things as communication and parenting skills, and were increasingly rooted in God through the teaching and encouragement from the pulpit. Although survival was often still mostly the focus, the Lord was always at least in their peripheral vision.

And so were others around them. Despite the overwhelming needs and demands in their own lives—or maybe *because* of them—Chuck and Susan began to feel a growing conviction to serve others.

So in the first year of their marriage, mired in unhealthy patterns of their own, overwhelmed with simply surviving, Chuck and Susan decided to join the Common Cause group for single parents. These were their reasons:

- They felt the gentle prodding of their God and church to do so;
- Their own life experiences deeply connected them with the needs of those people;
- If they didn't do it, it might not get done;
- Strangely, they felt their very lives depended upon doing so.

Although they had been informally serving others all along, the commitment to a Common Cause group called for additional sacrifices of time and energy. For Susan the move out of a Season of Life community group and into a Common Cause one was painful and slow. "I went kicking and screaming," she says. "The idea of ministry—serving others—was out of my comfort zone." In a sense, they forced themselves to serve.

They were surprised by the amount of time, energy, and sacrifice the ministry placed upon their lives; by the unsettling feelings of deep inadequacy; by the growing awareness that despite their best efforts, most of the single parent community's crying needs remained unmet.

Each year they wonder if this will be their last year with this Common Cause group. And each year they return. When pressed, they can't exactly tell you why. Mostly, they say, it is the only thing really worth doing. There is a mysterious satisfaction in experiencing the love of God and then, in whatever small and inadequate way you can, demonstrating that love to others. Underneath the pain and sacrifice of ministry are even greater surprises—a healing grace, a tenacious joy. Serving others, they say, has served them well.

In fact, serving others helped heal their marriage, even at a point when most everything else they tried to do caused it to crumble. Says Susan, "We needed to focus on somebody else besides ourselves." Says Chuck, "I could wallow in my self-pity and self-circumstances forever and never get any better, or I could go out and try to serve someone, however lamely I might do that." In the very act of serving has come the greatest amount of freedom and growth.

Sometimes the benefits of serving were immediate and obvious. For example, when Chuck and Susan helped organize a workshop on dealing with strong-willed children, they were the ones to benefit most. Originally designed to meet once a week for four weeks, the workshop was extended for more. Both Susan and Chuck entered into a counseling relationship with the teacher, and what they learned from him dramatically changed the way they related to their children. Wonderfully, over time, respect grew; and for the first time, healthy relationships slowly developed.

Just after his oldest daughter's marriage, his other daughter—the one who often had come home just to tell her father how much she hated him—gave him a phone call. His daughter's first words were: "Dad, do you have a Bible nearby?" This was also the same daughter who often told him that she didn't want anything to do with that "Christian crap." Chuck, nearly speechless, retrieved his Bible. "Now," she said, "could you turn to and read the story of the Prodigal Son?" After he read the story, his daughter broke down in tears. "Will you forgive me, Daddy?"

That was a turning point for Chuck. It showed him that God's power could be a bridge to the possible, even in the most impossible of situations, and that through serving others, you receive the most inexplicable and unexpected gifts. It is the very paradox that Jesus spoke so powerfully about in John 12:24, "I tell you the truth, unless a grain of wheat falls into the earth and dies, it remains by itself alone; but if it dies, it bears much fruit" (NASV).

LESSONS ABOUT LOVE

Today Chuck and Susan have many ministry stories to tell. Chuck loves the one about Mark, the eldest of three sons, whose father bailed out on them when they were very young. At one point, Mark was talking about suicide. His mother brought him to a car clinic, a ministry that the church operates for the benefit of low-income families, many of them single-parent homes. Mark did not want to be there. After his mother left, he sulked on a bench, scuffing his tennis shoes on the concrete. Chuck put his arm around Mark, and showed him the insides of an automobile—the place of combustion, horsepower, precision, and power.

In a very short time, Mark was alert, sparked with interest, humming with testosterone. As he looked around, he saw only males and tools and engines. On the edge of manhood himself, he felt—maybe for the first time in his life—the camaraderie of men.

After a few hours, Mark began to talk to Chuck about a few of the things in his life. After a few years, he was able to speak to Chuck from his soul—about his feelings of abandonment and, finally, about the small pinprick of hope he now had. Love, Chuck has learned, is not casually interested.

Susan's best friends are Mary and Brenda. They have been together as single parents for years and years. Early in their friendship, they would plug the holes in each other's lives—their missing men, their children's often empty searches, the string of lonely, lonely hours. Together, they laughed and cried and, when they could find the energy and courage, prayed. Mary, once married and once divorced, got pregnant out of wedlock. Susan was there for the labor and delivery of her godchild, Kate, who is now eleven. Love, Susan has learned, is not about what string to pull. It is about being there.

Chuck and Susan have dozens of stories like this. Few have tidy endings. The human struggle to live and love well as a Christian in an often cruel world does not always feel like you just won the lottery. It's not like those sappy love songs, either. The only real match for the toxicity of sin, layer upon layer upon layer, is the matchless and blood-smeared grace of God.

But that is not the end of it, they say. On the bridge between their own need and the sacrificial service they give to others, moves the strangest feeling: joy.

When you ask them to explain, they can't quite find the words. The only way to understand it, they say, is to experience it for yourself.

CHAPTER 8

URBAN ENTREPRENEUR

Command those who are rich in this present world . . .

to do good, to be rich in good deeds, and to

be generous and willing to share.

—1 Timothy 6:17–18

A BRIDGE STORY

Newspapers called it the "Dance of Danger"— bridge construction on top of swaying catwalks and high towers, sometimes hundreds of feet in the air, blown by ill winds. This dance had even yielded a calculated fatality rate: For each one million dollars spent, one life would be lost. That was what one could expect.

Engineers of the Golden Gate Bridge, however, believed the risks could be lowered. When construction began in 1932, numerous safety measures were put into place and strictly enforced: mandatory use of hard hats, prescription filtered eye glasses, no showboating (cause for automatic firing), tie-off lines, and an on-site hospital helped to greatly reduce the casualty rate. After nearly four years of construction and $20 million spent, only one worker had died.

The most effective safety device, without question, was as new to bridge building as it was old to the circus: the use of a trapeze net. Costing $130,000, *this large net draped sixty feet below the roadbed under construction, extending ten feet to either side. So effective was the safety net that the newspapers began running box scores: "Score on the Gate Bridge Safety Net to Date: 8 Lives Saved!" Those men whose lives had been delivered by the net were said to have joined the "Halfway to Hell Club."*

Beyond that, the net had another significant benefit: it freed many of the workers from an often paralyzing sense of fear. And that, many said, helped them work more productively.

BUD FINLEY WAS TEN when Little Rock's Central High School was integrated. He would sit at the supper table and hear his father talk about the situation in language peppered with racial slurs. Growing up, Bud believed this prejudice was just the way things were—a kind of natural and unquestioned fact like cherries on a cherry tree.

When Bud was in junior high, integration began at Hall High School, also in Little Rock, where his sister was attending. One morning he wrote a note and stuck it in his pocket: *"Go to hell niggers."* He meant to drop it out the passenger window at the school when he and his mother picked up his sister after school, but he forgot. The next day his mother found the note in his pants, and his father, with a heavy-handed hypocrisy, gave him a spanking.

Bud was confused. He was an eighth grader with raging hormones and an unquestioned devotion to the Rebel Flag and the song "Dixie." His excuse was simply that he was trained to be that way. Never once did he stop to think what it would be like to be one of those black students and live through that terrible ordeal.

Over time Bud believed he had shed his racism, or at least its ugly external carcass. He was tolerant of progress and talk of civil rights—up to a point. He became a Christian, and he knew he shouldn't hate anyone. Yet in his heart, he suspected this: he would no more associate with a black person than he would handle a snake. In Bud's world, bridges were mostly painted lily white.

But that was about to change.

Nearly three decades after the integration of Central High, Bud agreed to be a part of a "Helping Hands" community service project with our church. Bud was assigned to help at an inner-city housing project named Eastgate. He could live with that. Rake a few leaves. Tell a few jokes. Pick up some trash. And go home at five. It might even make him feel good, make him sleep well for a night or two. Convince him that he wasn't still a racist.

Michael was seven and black and sweet. Bud started messing around with him that day, telling jokes, throwing fake punches like a boxer. When the day was over, Bud asked Michael if he could come visit him every once in a while. Michael agreed.

Within a week, they loved each other.

Bud mentored Michael for the next three years. But it was Bud who was to learn the most. As he related to Michael as a person—and not as a member of a needy class or a persecuted race—the scales began to fall from his eyes. The scales were reptilian, cold-blooded, and when they were finally gone, he could see the pumping of his racist and diseased heart.

He could no longer bask in the warmth of his "good works." Without love, they amounted to no more than a clanging cymbal.

THRIVING ON CHALLENGE

Bud Finley admits he is a bit of a paradox. On the one hand, he is conservative. He was unimpressed with the cultural revolution of the 1960s. He wouldn't know cannabis from cocklebur. He has the same bland image that he had in high school.

On the other hand, he is a man given to addiction. Not to drugs or chocolate or golf, but to thrill, to adrenaline, to a driving purpose. Underneath his pin-striped Croft & Barrows shirts beats a wild man's heart.

Some might call it craving. Some might call it passion. It is probably both.

Bud knows himself well enough to live with the reality that he is a self-described "Rush Junkie." In looking back over his life, he sees that the pursuit of adrenaline, more times than not, has determined his life paths. He thrives on challenge, extremes, and the incessant and obsessive avoidance of routine.

In his twenties he grew a beard, moved with his wife to a farm, and bought a slaughterhouse. That business failed, but he thrived on the edge. He got involved in brokering deals for the newly deregulated savings and loan industry, and eventually started his own real estate company, dealing in mortgages. When he began working with cellular phone companies to find sites to build towers on, he intuitively knew of the great potential. At the time, he could hardly even spell *telecommunications*. Bud contracted with a regional cellular phone company, and the next thing he knew, he had a company doing $12 million a year with more than seventy-five employees across the country. His annual salary, at times, reached $1 million.

By most people's standards, Bud Finley had certainly arrived. With diligence, perseverance, luck, and love of challenge, he had made it, whatever "it" was. By external appearances, he was successful—wealthy, with a respected family. Yet something was still troubling him.

There was a nearly constant sense of being preoccupied—a nagging feeling that his worth was only as sound as the next deal and that the next deal was elusive, continually just out of reach. He resented the fact that the wheel needed constant turning. The preoccupation sapped his energy, demanded his focus. He regretted sacrificing the deeper needs of his family in order to feed his preoccupation. While he was able to spend wonderful times with his three boys, he never found the time to go deeper, to "really teach them." If they learned, it was because they watched. Focus demanded compromise. He was involved with his family but rarely deeply and intimately connected.

Spiritually, he was slick. He read the right books. He said the right words. Bill Bright, head of Campus Crusade for Christ, spoke at his company. He witnessed and studied, prayed and tithed. In his community group at Fellowship Bible Church, he developed strong bonds, speaking openly and honestly about important life issues.

But deep inside his heart, during the quietest moments, a restlessness would seize him. Even in his most devout moments, he discovered a nagging absorption with his own selfish interests.

As Fellowship Bible Church began gearing up for Common Cause groups—for the building of bridges to the unbelieving community— Bud was intrigued. The call for a risky, creative, and compelling faith seemed right to him; it touched his entrepreneurial soul. Yet his attempts at ministry always seemed to be the equivalent of lip-syncing a gospel song: he always had the sense he was faking it. He could never find an inroad into any form of spiritual passion.

Little did he understand at the time that God was orchestrating deep change in his life, the greatest of which was about to unfold. The man who had, as a child, written a note saying "niggers go to hell" was about to have his world and life transformed by a small black child living in the inner city.

ENTERING INTO MICHAEL'S WORLD

Bud, the millionaire, and Michael, the poor black child. At first the novelty of the relationship fueled Bud's need for adrenaline, the rush of a calculated headfirst jump into the unknown. He got a charge out of going into a McDonald's in the poorest part of town with a young black boy.

But no matter the motivation. Over the bridge of a growing and shared love, Bud entered into Michael's world. And that changed everything.

Slowly, he began to do what he never even contemplated as a racist junior high student: to understand firsthand what it is like to be young, black, and poor with little more than a ghost of a chance. He saw Michael's squalid apartment, where as many as eleven people lived at any one time. He befriended Michael's mother, who despite having children with three absent fathers, cared and nurtured her young ones with a deep love. In this neighborhood, he saw the thirteen-year-old girls with their babies. In Michael's confession of dashed dreams, he heard about the parties, wild with booze, drugs, and loud music. Bud learned to joke with the deadbeat dads.

On the outside—from an unbridged distance—it would have been easy to reduce Michael's poverty to a simple stereotype or two. He could have left, inside of his white skin, with feelings of superiority, humble pride, and enough excuses to build a fence, not a bridge. But he couldn't. He had come to love Michael, and love always seeks understanding. He began to listen as much as teach.

After spending three years with Michael, Bud came to a deeper understanding of the oppressive cycle of hopelessness and disconnected charity. In Michael's world, the future did not exist, and the past often had to be blocked out.

In Michael's neighborhood, opportunity almost never came to knock.

Bud would take Michael to common places, which Michael would find peculiar, almost exotic. When he arrived at Bud's farm, Michael saw horses, a pond, woods. He could fish, jump on a trampoline, and swim. You would have thought he had just been to Disney World. What his children took as commonplace, sometimes boring, Michael had never even dreamed existed.

The third or fourth time he tutored Michael at school, Michael asked, "Bud, what day does your check come?" Confused, Bud asked him three times what he meant. Finally, it hit him. Michael was speaking of welfare checks. That's the way Michael thought people got money.

Bud tried to expand Michael's vision. One day he drove Michael to his friend's construction company site. When Bud showed him what a bricklayer did, it was a revelation, a peephole into a different world.

As they crisscrossed each other's worlds, a realization began to dawn on Bud. If you are white and real smart, you are destined for good fortune; if you are black and real smart, you will probably be okay; if you are white and not so smart, you will get by; but if you are black and not so smart, you haven't even got a prayer. The cycle, left unbroken, is destined to repeat itself.

And despair—born of a life without a safety net—is a powerful, paralyzing force.

A GROWING PASSION

As Michael opened his world to him, questions began to form in Bud's mind: How could the love of Christ penetrate the inner-city community? How could it provide an antidote to the poison of welfare with its bureaucratic and deadly tendencies toward dehumanization? How could the love of God dissolve seemingly impenetrable barriers of systematic, engrained, and long-standing hate between race and class?

Bud began to seek help from directors of different social agencies in Little Rock. Soon he found himself on three or four local agency boards, and he was beginning to understand the dynamics of the city's social service network.

As it turned out, it wasn't much of a network. Each agency was mostly on its own: operated by loving, dedicated professionals; understaffed; underfunded. As Bud circulated between the agencies, he saw duplication of services and lack of interagency communication.

Despite these obstacles, the agencies often did a tremendous job. In the summer of 1998, Bud and his wife assumed legal guardianship of a seventeen-year-old black youth who had been nurtured by one such agency. Despite a chaotic family life, the young man is stellar in almost every regard—a 3.0 grade point average, articulate, a loving Christian, and popular with the girls. He is a living testimony to the power of social service.

Bud's entrepreneurial mind whirled. In his mind, there are always greater possibilities. What if, for example, the black director of this agency could meet up with the white director of that agency? And what if, between the two of them, they could find ways to work together and reduce duplication of efforts. And if he could get two together, how about three or four, or even the entire community of social service agencies? After all, they shared the same love of children and the same desire to break the cycles of despair and hopelessness. Why couldn't they, in a movement toward that same goal, share other things?

In 1996 I took Bud with me to attend a conference in California featuring management guru Peter Drucker. At the conference Drucker spoke about the desperate need for leadership and integration in inner-city social service agencies—giving a formal voice to many of the same ideas that Bud had already been kicking around. Most agency directors, Drucker said, were by nature "lovers, not leaders"—excellent at hands-on ministry. Unfortunately, they spend most of their energies on myriad moments of service rather than the development of a composite, single Big Picture. That was fine. They were doing what they were good at doing. But, Drucker said, "What if strong leadership was brought in to help provide an overall vision, to synchronize the work of different agencies, and to recruit and coordinate the enormous resources of the business and church communities?"

For perhaps the first time in his life, Bud, on the spot, felt an awesome sense of God's will. This was *it*, he knew. This was what he *had* to do. The bell of spiritual passion was ringing in his ears. As he looks back, Bud can see that God was orchestrating the pieces of his life, carefully preparing him for this particular ministry. It wasn't by accident, for example, that he:

- was raised in an environment of racism, fully understanding its bitter and persistent venom;
- was successfully entrepreneurial, paving a path of experience and resources;
- met Michael, who in an environment of mutual charity, gave him a priceless gift: an unprejudiced understanding of his inner-city world;

- was a member of a church that, over a ten-year-period, deeply exposed him to biblical teaching and challenged him in the radical, life-transforming, world-changing love of Christ.

The adrenaline was flowing, but this time—for the first time—it pumped all the way into his soul.

A PASSION FULLY FIRED

In 1997 Bud sold his consulting business. While he continued to work, he used part of the money—$2 million—to establish a foundation for urban ministry under the umbrella of Fellowship Bible Church. Initially, $250,000 was given away to nonprofit agencies. The remaining $1.75 million was deposited in fixed-income investments and now generates about $120,000 a year. Enough money, he believed, to hire a director and an administrative assistant and begin assisting local social service agencies.

The goals would be simple:

- provide consultation;
- upgrade services;
- attract resources from corporations and churches;
- work to synchronize social service work.

Bud knew execution would be difficult. But he has always loved the ring of the word "impossible."

Shortly after establishing the foundation, twenty-one different agencies—both secular and religious—were invited to a luncheon to explain its goals. During that meeting, the question was asked: "How many of you would like someone to come alongside you and, at no charge, provide planning and organizational assistance?" Most responded positively. Most understood—and welcomed—the need for vision and strategy. That provided a starting point.

Bud also investigated models around the country. In Memphis, for example, he discovered that the Memphis Leadership Foundation had been in existence for more than twelve years. Started with just one staff member, the foundation was generating several million dollars a year in funds for inner-city agencies from businesses and churches, and it had established a synchronized network of housing, banking, food, and vocational programs. It could be done.

When Bud speaks of his dream, which he does now at the drop of a hat, he does so in the context of the singular. His vision, while large, is always rooted in the context of one individual. He envisioned a network of social agencies, businesses, and churches working together to provide an integrated web of services so that a child—from cradle until independence—could benefit from interconnected encouragement, assistance, and tools. Through loving, one-on-one relationships, a child could expand his or her vision, and learn how to reach for new dreams. The end result: a tiny—but huge—break in the chain of despair.

There was only one problem with Bud's dream. It wasn't quite big enough. What he failed to understand was that God had an even bigger dream for his life.

After the foundation was established, the elders of Fellowship appointed Bud, Jim Strawn, and myself to the board of directors. The search for a leader to head up the work of assisting inner-city agencies quickly began in earnest. After almost a year of fruitless searches nationwide, it became clear to all of us that we really needed two people: an entrepreneur who could provide big picture leadership to this new venture, *and* a networker/consultant who could interface person-to-person with local service agencies.

Ironically, the latter appeared before the former. Shelby Smith, a black banker from Jackson, Mississippi, became our consensus pick as the networker/consultant who would also serve as day-to-day manager of the organization. But where could we find the high-level executive director we needed to lead this new enterprise?

After a number of failed interviews and frustrating dead-ends, a board meeting suddenly was transformed into holy ground through a simple question.

"What about you, Bud?"

On May 5, 1999, Bud Finley went all the way. He left his job and is now executive director of "Urban Strategies," the foundation's new name. Although he still works some in real estate and the cattle business, there is no question where Bud's heart lies.

He and Shelby Smith have set off to change our community one life at a time. "Never," Bud says, "have I experienced a rush like this one." Yes, there is fear. Real fear. The kind that could paralyze a man's soul.

But underneath him, Bud senses *a divine safety net* has been drawn up by God himself. And that has freed him to pursue his dreams with an unshakable confidence.

PART FOUR

EXPANDING THE i^2 EFFORT

New Partnerships,

New Adventures

CHAPTER 9

JOINING WITH OTHER CHURCHES

Two are better than one . . .

—Ecclesiastes 4:9

What if the 21st century was more than the dawn of a new millennium? What if, for the churches of central Arkansas, it commenced a new spirit of cooperation? What if pastors reached out to one another, embracing one another in love, no longer competing with, but supporting one another, praying with one another, crying out to God for their community, working together? What if?

—ShareFest Video Script

A BRIDGE STORY

In the great bridge collapses of the nineteenth and early twentieth centuries, pride has often been the culprit, with deadly results. By some accounts, as many as one in four bridges collapsed. That is probably exaggerated. But still the point is well taken: as commerce expanded in this new age of mobility and the demand for more bridges increased, people were dying. In the attitude of one engineer, "Build it by the mile and cut it off by the yard" became a dangerous equation of economy at the expense of good judgment.

In 1845, Robert Stephenson's Dee Bridge, the longest metal truss built to that date, buckled, *claiming five lives. In 1879, Thomas Bouch's Tay Bridge over Scotland's Firth of Tay went down in a gale, killing seventy-five people. In 1907, the collapse of Quebec Bridge over the St. Lawrence in Canada caused the death of another seventy-five.*

All of these disasters, experts now believe, could have and should have been prevented. Engineers and bridge companies—often working in isolation, competition, and the pursuit of reputation and money—were simply negligent. Their failure to cooperate with others, to seek help and assistance, and, where appropriate, to work together became the tragic downfall of their bridge-building efforts.

- *Isolation*
- *Competition*
- *Pursuit of reputation*

These, not the lack of competence or skill, proved to be the real enemies of bridge building.

"**THERE IS A WIDENING** gap between the condition of the average American city and the impact and influence of the church," observes Jack Dennison in his fine book, *City Reaching.* "When the church measures itself against its past, there may be a degree of satisfaction found in growing numbers. But when looked at in light of an increasing population, accelerating decay and the greater needs of our cities, we find the church's capacity to affect change continues to plummet. We are losing our cities at an increasing rate."[1]

I wonder how many churches would be truly alarmed at this statement? The fact is, many churches have long abandoned any idea of reaching and influencing the city in which they are nestled, settling instead on some *reduced* vision that is much less intimidating. In this regard, Doug Small warns, "Pastors have given themselves to ministering only to the pain of their congregations but have failed to mobilize their congregations to minister to the pain and problems of the city. Either we learn to do both or reaching our cities for Christ will be nothing more than a hope and dream."[2]

Biblically speaking, the "reach" Jesus originally had in mind for his church began with nothing less than a city. "You will be my witnesses *in Jerusalem,* and in all Judea and Samaria, and to the ends of the earth" (Acts 1:8, italics added). The game plan described here for the church is clear: *city,* region, and world. Churches in the New Testament were named for the city they belonged to: "church of the Thessalonians" (1 Thessalonians 1:1); "church of the Laodiceans" (Colossians 4:16); "church of God in Corinth" (1 Corinthians 1:2); "church in Ephesus" (Revelation 2:1); and so on. Surely, this naming implied a calling with it too! When Jesus originally described his church, he pictured it in terms of storming the gates of a city (Matthew 16:18). Clearly, "city reaching" is a biblical concept. It is what the church, at ground level, is to be about.

> *So how does a church with a biblical vision of irresistible influence reach a whole city? The answer is, not alone!*

So how does a church with a biblical vision of irresistible influence reach a whole city? The answer is, *not alone!* No matter how large and influential a church might be in a local community, that church represents only a small part of the body of Christ. And as good as its bridge-building efforts may be, its impact will be, at best, limited. No one church can effectively reach a city! The city is too large, too diverse, too complex, for any one ember from Christ's redemptive fire to light the way.

BUT WHAT IF . . .

What if there were a way to not only turn churches outward but also to *join them together* in unity of purpose?

Five years ago if you would have proposed that to me, I would have balked with more than a little skepticism. The closest thing to any form of church unity in Little Rock was a monthly pastoral alliance luncheon, which had mercifully passed away years ago.

But two things changed that. Two simple but very powerful things. In what we now believe has been a Holy Spirit–directed process, the churches of central Arkansas are slowly beginning to find a way back to one another and a way forward to our cities.

What are these two change agents that gave us this new, but real hope?

- The new relational unity we established through *prayer* together.
- The new credibility we established through *serving our community* together.

We are discovering that nothing brings churches together in a city better than prayer and good works.

We are discovering that nothing brings churches together in a city better than prayer and good works. Suspended by these two towers, a broader and more powerful bridge of spiritual influence is now being constructed in our area to the glory of God. And with that construction, I sense that something very New Testament is happening: The churches *in* Little Rock and North Little Rock are beginning to feel like the Church *of* Little Rock and North Little Rock. As different as many of us are, we are developing a spiritually authentic common ground.

OUR NEW RELATIONAL UNITY THROUGH PRAYER

For many years God has stirred the hearts of a few faithful men and women to pray that churches in our community would come together in unity. I have no doubt that during those long, barren years they wondered if God would ever grant them what their hearts so fervently longed for. Still, they prayed.

In 1995 the first signs of an answer began to appear. First, a small group of pastors began praying together in North Little Rock. They had no other agenda except to beseech God together for their lives and for their people. At about the same time, in our own church, God began to move us to the concept of i², and one of our staff pastors, Ray Williams, was convicted of the need to network with other churches.

As our church geared up over the next several years to equip people to build bridges into the community, Ray joined what was now a growing prayer network of pastors around central Arkansas. In early 1997 he began reading about the work of International Renewal Ministry (IRM), based in Portland, Oregon, which had helped facilitate prayer movements among pastors and other Christian leaders in more than a hundred and fifty cities around the world.

Their focus was simple yet powerful: Get pastors away to pray, with no other agenda than seeking the Lord Jesus together, and wonderful things will happen. They will build relationships that last and find their common ground in the Good Shepherd.

When Ray asked me if I would attend a four-day prayer retreat facilitated by IRM in January 1998, I must confess to being both hesitant and cynical. As a rule, pastors are overwhelmed with invitations like this that sound good but usually go nowhere. "This will never work," I thought to myself. Besides, like so many others, I was already overburdened with the urgent needs and nonstop pressures from my own church. *Four days?*

While reluctantly agreeing to go, I told Ray I had a hard time seeing much of a strategic benefit in this. I doubted we would become real. More than likely, I feared, it would be four days of subtle (and not so subtle) pastoral competition and comparison.

I could not have been more wrong. Through a deep brokenness, we united in and around the grace of God. God's presence at times was almost "touchable." Rarely have I witnessed such an outpouring of shared pain, passion, and confession. And this was among pastors! It was a retreat, I am convinced, that dug the first footings for building an authentic unity among pastors who often don't relate well to one another.

Pastors, by and large, are isolated people consumed with playing a role and meeting the endless needs of people. Outside of church events, conferences, and speaking engagements, which often fail to emphasize the building of true relationships, many pastors are lonely people. They often feel they have few people they can really talk to. In a superstar culture of larger churches, pastors become more inaccessible, and their communication to church members is mostly instructional, moving always in the direction of higher to lower.

Most pastors live by an unspoken rule: Guard against being too transparent; play your position. As a result, the image can quickly swallow up the reality. If you are a pastor, you know what I mean.

So when our prayer retreat started on the first day by singing old hymns, I wondered how honest and real we would get. Many of us knew each other only in passing or by what we had read in the newspaper about one another. Those who had planned and prayed for the retreat were a bit more optimistic, but we all faced a nervous awkwardness in the face of so many unstated divisions: denomination, size of church, race, doctrinal beliefs, projected images, and assumptions. And then there was that fear of the inevitable pecking order.

By design, the first day of the retreat, which was mediated by the International Renewal Ministry, focused on the person of Christ in praise and prayer. Focusing on the power, majesty, and incomparable person of God helped break down the barriers we had carefully and subtly erected to keep us apart. In a common and powerful worship of the Creator God, a floodgate of relational authenticity was soon released in a river of tears.

Titles, images, perceptions, and preconceived notions began to crumble in the common ground of that holy place. The next day, through prayers, we each began to release what was *really* on our hearts: hurts, disappointments, guilt, victories, failures, and the sustaining call of God. It was such a relief to hear these men talk openly of the same things I often felt as a pastor.

On the second morning, a pastor shared how he had yet to forgive God for the recent death of his son. In the middle of the room a chair was placed, and one by one, each pastor shared from the soul. And one by one, each pastor was surrounded and prayed for. There was an abundance of tears, hugging, and touching. The Holy Spirit created a powerful sense of brokenness, of deep humility, of the common and unyielding bond of the grace of God.

What about the inevitable question of doctrine, you may be asking? I am not saying that doctrinal differences didn't or shouldn't matter. Nothing could be further from the truth. But it is difficult to maintain the separation caused by many "nonessential" doctrinal divisions once you have heard another man, divinely called to ministry, broken before God, praying his heart out. It becomes almost impossible not to acknowledge a brother in Christ. And, if he is a brother, despite some differences in opinion, can we truly continue to pretend to be strangers in the work of the kingdom?

In the pursuit of doctrinal purity—the admirable and necessary goal of theological orthodoxy—I have tended to emphasize truth over love. It seems I am forever learning that a delicate balance of both is critical. At this first prayer retreat, one of the ministers, an Eastern Orthodox priest, did not participate in communion because of his theological belief. Although he politely left the room, a nervous energy ran among the other participants. Another communion was scheduled on our final night together. What should we do? In respect to him, we decided to forgo it. Did we compromise the Word of God? On this occasion, I believe we *fulfilled* it by "giving preference to another in honor" (Romans 12:10 NASV).

So powerful and humbling was the Spirit of God those four days that, at the suggestion of the IRM representatives, we elected eight men to serve on a leadership team that would continue our efforts. Such an action is usually not considered that early. That kind of humility—pastors electing other pastors for leadership—usually requires much more time.

Across central Arkansas today, under the leadership of what is now called the "Nehemiah Group," a growing network of pastoral prayer cells is developing. Once a month those cells unite in a citywide prayer meeting. And we continue to hold our annual four-day prayer retreat.

What have we learned? First and foremost, we have learned to respect one another. In some cases, that respect has risen to genuine admiration. Our prayer-based relationships have also paved the ground for loving one another. Pastors are beginning to call each other in crises, share information and services, exchange pulpits, and join their congregations together around common projects. Churches are now even financially investing in one another! I know of one instance where two churches, once fierce competitors, experienced a miraculous healing when one church gave a significant financial contribution to the building campaign of the other. Does this sound like the church we read about in the New Testament? Absolutely.

OUR NEW CREDIBILITY THROUGH SERVING OUR COMMUNITY

Whereas prayer became the catalyst for a new unity between our churches, good works have become a catalyst for building a new credibility with our community.

This did not happen easily, however. In my own heart, God had been leading me to dream about the possibility of expanding i² to other churches. Even with the success we as a church had had in building bridges of proof to our city, it had become clear to me that no one church alone could reach our community with the impact envisioned in Matthew 5:16. No one church had enough "light" to do this. It would take churches miraculously becoming *one* (John 17:21) and turning outward in selfless love to bring this about. As Jack Dennison reminds us, "If the church in the city has any hope of truly impacting the city and its societies, it will require the collective effort of the entire Church."[3]

So as our prayer network brought more and more churches together, it seemed right to approach the Nehemiah Group about organizing a giant cooperative effort in serving and stirring our community. I called it "ShareFest."

Immediately, I understood my mistake. I had jumped the gun; I was moving too fast. Some complained that my idea was only tactical—just another event—untethered to any overall strategy. Others felt it would misdirect the group from its primary mission of prayer. Still others said it was too great in size and scope and thus too risky.

I could see and feel the tension rising in the group. For these men, gathered under the premise of praying together, it felt like a power move. *Here comes the megachurch pastor to take control.* It was a relational disaster.

Ray Williams (chairman of the Nehemiah Group) and I immediately called for another meeting in which the primary agenda was simple: my apology. I told these men I had blown it. I told them I valued our relationships far more than any tasks we might do together. I withdrew my idea and told them it was dead unless one of them decided to resurrect it sometime in the future.

And almost a year later, one of them did. In a half-day of prayer and interaction about where God was leading the Nehemiah Group, three themes emerged:

- We needed to continue to strengthen and grow our prayer network.
- We needed a way to document the true needs of our community and a way to assess the true condition of our churches overall. (Chapter 11 tells how we accomplished this.)
- We needed some way to make an impact on the community with a visible demonstration of the love of God. We concluded that our city would no longer listen to the church unless we could demonstrate that we were for real.

But how? As discussion ensued around this last theme, someone suggested we revisit my ShareFest idea. Suddenly everyone seemed excited. Eager. "How good and pleasant it is when brothers live together in unity!" (Psalm 133:1). God was at work and we knew it.

ShareFest was never intended to be just an event. No one wants or needs another event that disappears as quickly as it came. Through ShareFest we desired a whole new beginning for the churches of central Arkansas. ShareFest would be our catalyst for launching a movement that would help turn our churches outward:

- To our neighbors
- To new partnerships with the community
- To real needs

The idea was simple. Assemble as many churches as possible and *light up* (Matthew 5:16) the central Arkansas community with as many good works as possible in a concentrated period of time. Don't preach. Prove! Serve! Give! Love! Put flesh on the Word of God. Make it tangible, observable, and undeniable. For a whole week, do these things as humbly and as authentically as we know how. Then walk away, asking nothing in return. Finally, repeat this week every year until our churches discover a better way to build a bridge that incarnates Christ's love and grace to our community.

SHAREFEST: BEYOND OUR WILDEST DREAMS

Over time our initial ideas began to take shape. We decided to invite churches to partner with us in the following ways over one week in November:

First, each church would commit to *planning and implementing a significant service project* of its choice somewhere in the community, preferably in one of the neighborhoods adjacent to the church. The key word in this first objective was "significant"—as opposed to "token." We were asking each church to sacrificially turn out and give of themselves in a way that would leave a meaningful and lasting mark of love. As such, the projects needed to be focused, well-planned, and, financially speaking, sacrificial. They could, for example, refurbish a park, a school, a boys and girls club. Build a Habitat home. Rebuild a playground. Come alongside a needy social service agency and take on a major project important to them. Work with a local neighborhood association in the inner city. Repair homes for the poor and elderly. Whatever service project a church chose, the goal was to make an impact.

Second, we would ask each church to *participate in "ShareFest Village," a Sunday afternoon cooperative effort that would allow local church members "to bless" certain preselected social service agencies.* For instance, you could come to ShareFest Village and bring food for the hungry that would be distributed through the Arkansas Rice Depot or Here's Life Inner City. Or you could come and give blood to the American Red Cross. You could donate children's coats to the Salvation Army or toys to the Marine Corp's Toys for Tots program. You could sign an organ donor card with ARORA. Or you could do it all. But in this afternoon of sharing, we were asking the sponsoring churches to do it *together.* Together our contributions would be a concentrated, significant statement to our community.

Third, we would ask each church to *participate in an evening of unity.* Churches would cancel their regular Sunday evening activities and gather instead at a local arena for an evening of worship and prayer. We would pray for the needs of our community; we would pray over our city and state political leaders (whom we would invite); and we would pray that our churches would once again be a vital force in our community.

We would also take a "love offering" on this evening for our community, to be divided equally among several preselected social service agencies that:

- are widely known as a servant of the community
- have an established track record of organizational excellence and integrity
- are "faith based" or closely allied with Christian values
- are addressing the needs of families and/or youth
- are clearly getting results in these areas
- had been interviewed and approved by the Nehemiah Group

Finally, we would ask each sponsoring church to *help financially underwrite ShareFest with an advance contribution.* Our hope was that the expenses for ShareFest could be met months ahead of time.

Was this plan bold? Audacious? Daring? Crazy? The answer is Yes. Nevertheless, the Nehemiah Group set the plan in motion in April of 1999. We rented Alltel Arena, which at the time was still under construction. We set the week before Thanksgiving, November 15–21, as our date for this concentrated outpouring of light. And we began to pray that God would give us fifty churches, a faith stretch to be sure, since at the time we did not have a commitment from a single church.

ShareFest became, in the months that followed, an unsettling effort of faith, prayers, and a ton of hard work. It soon became clear it was bigger than what the Nehemiah Group could handle on its own. Therefore, an administrative team was formed to coordinate the enormous number of people and activities it would require. But it was also right here that we caught our first glimpse of God's favor and blessing. How? By those God raised up to form our administrative team. They were not ordinary laypeople. They were extraordinary leaders whom God sovereignly put in our path to bring these dreams to reality. By the time ShareFest finally took place, Rick Caldwell (ShareFest's executive director), Mona Thompson, Gary Jones, Paul Stevens, and Elaine Garrett were giving a Herculean faith effort to a daring possibility that was never a certain success.

But ShareFest did succeed—beyond our wildest dreams. And not just as an event, but as the beginning of a movement.

The fifty churches we prayed so diligently for on the front end actually surpassed one hundred churches by the time ShareFest began. Businesses as well as churches joined the effort. The state newspaper, the *Arkansas Democrat-Gazette,* provided much needed promotion at no cost. A major food distributor donated tons of food. A production company coordinated our Alltel worship and prayer service.

> *But ShareFest did succeed— beyond our wildest dreams. And not just as an event, but as the beginning of a movement.*

Officially, the community saw our churches perform more than 105 service projects. On Saturday alone more than three thousand Christian volunteers were out loving their neighbors, doing everything from building homes, to landscaping, to painting and remodeling the interior of an elementary school, to putting in a new basketball court at an inner-city YMCA.

Wanda Barry, a mother of three whose husband has been in a wheelchair for the last nine years after an accidental shooting, cried while her husband received the ceremonial key to their new house.

Ronda Jones, who volunteered to help build that house, even struggling to nail down shingles on a roof, started to nail down a secret to the Christian life: that real faith lies outside one's own comfort zone.

An elderly widow, living in a dilapidated house that was far beyond repair, was simply overjoyed, mostly for the company, when several volunteers showed up at her home to replace her front porch.

The first-grade teacher at Pike View Elementary School said she couldn't believe the incredible changes that hundreds of church volunteers made in her school. "Our kids have a new school," she said beaming. "If Christianity were more like this, people would be interested. I know I would."

On Sunday afternoon, thousands turned out at the ShareFest Village. Even before the doors were opened, our projected goal for food gathering had already been met and exceeded. The American Red Cross, according to Director Mike Ferell, was "crazy busy" dealing with the record number of blood donations that were being given. "This is the largest three-day blood donation in the history of our region," he said.

FIRST ASSEMBLY OF GOD: A BRIDGE-BUILDING CHURCH

Their faces said it all. On Monday morning, November 22, 1999, the students of Pike View Elementary School in North Little Rock arrived to a school that had undergone a miraculous transformation over the weekend. With wide eyes they looked in awe at the refurbished playground, the brightly colored murals, the newly shined hallways . . . everything seemed different. One child exclaimed, "Is this a new school?"

No, it was the same building. But over ShareFest weekend, nearly 300 members of First Assembly of God in North Little Rock had moved in and made it *seem* like new.

Pike View Elementary was built in 1962. Like many public schools in central Arkansas, it has trouble getting the money it needs to maintain the building. So when First Assembly decided to participate in ShareFest, they chose to focus their efforts on one, strategic project.

Under the leadership of Senior Pastor Alvin Garrison and Pastor Rod Loy, church members approached Pike View Principal Diane Crites and said they would like to make as many repairs and improvements to the school as they could in one weekend. "When I told her what we wanted to do," Loy says, "she said she had never heard of anything like this."

With her approval, they asked each teacher to submit a "wish list." The church designated $10,000 for the project, and enlisted area businesses to donate another $10,000 in materials. Employees of some of those businesses also volunteered their services.

Early Saturday morning, volunteers converged on the school. In addition to the projects already mentioned, in one day they:

- Replaced landscaping around the school
- Built and installed 70 cabinet units in classrooms
- Renovated existing shelves
- Painted all interior and exterior doors
- Installed new electrical outlets in every classroom

- Repaired all the lavatories
- Put in a new tile floor in the offices
- Tore out old radiators that hadn't been used for years
- Thoroughly cleaned the entire building
- Cooked and served lunch for all volunteers plus hundreds of people from the neighborhood

Pike View teachers and administrators were stunned by the scope of the refurbishing project. One first-grade teacher said, "Nobody's ever done anything like this for us before." And Principal Crites said, "I think this is the most fabulous day of my life as far as education is concerned. I've been in this 29 years and this is the first time a community or church project has come through for us."

First Assembly's motivations were summarized in a banner in front of the school proclaiming, "Because We Care: 'Love one another as I have loved you.' John 13:34." As church member Kathy Brockinton said, "This is our way of showing the love of Jesus, because Jesus ministered to people on a practical level. What He did was not abstract. He didn't just preach; He met their needs where they were and this is what the kids need."

Senior Pastor Garrison obviously had the vision for bridge building when he said, "What we are doing is demonstrating the love of Jesus to people who need to feel that love. . .and that's what it's all about: acts of kindness to build a bridge from our heart to theirs. We are joining together, letting this community know that Jesus loves them, that we love them, and that First Assembly loves them."

A number of members at First Assembly remarked that they couldn't remember the church doing anything so significant. And Loy notes, "We've never done anything that got us more attention." In fact, people from the area told First Assembly members that they wanted to begin going to their church.

The day was so successful that First Assembly wants to choose a new school to refurbish each year. Loy's main problem is that so many church members already want to help that "we may overwhelm one school," he says. "Perhaps we need to do two."

The Alltel Arena evening of unity was equally impressive. Over 7,000 people attended, including Arkansas Governor Mike Huckabee, Little Rock Mayor Jim Daily, and North Little Rock Mayor Patrick Henry Hays.

Earlier in the week, Governor Huckabee had said, "It is the work of the church which makes possible what never could be accomplished by a governmental agency. A check will never substitute for a church." That night, amidst the worship and prayer, he summed up ShareFest in one word—"Stunning." Mayor Daily compared the gathering to "a temple for God."

We prayed over city officials, showed videos reviewing the week's activities, took up a love offering, and spent significant time in worship and praise. People huddled in small groups to petition God for the needs and problems of our community—racism, poverty, healing of families, help for our schools, and many other concerns.

But perhaps the most dramatic moment was when Bill Elliff, pastor of the Summit Church, stepped forward. On behalf of the churches participating in ShareFest, Bill delivered a public confession of our failure to be the church Jesus envisioned. He also offered a public commitment to do better in the new millennium. What he said is worth reprinting here in its entirety:

OUR CONFESSION

Realizing Christ's prayer is for all of his children to walk in unity with him and each other (John 17), we humbly confess . . .

- Our *jealousy and envy* which has led to competition instead of cooperation.
- Our *prejudice* which has perverted the true picture of Christ's perfect love and acceptance.
- Our *pride* which has led us to exalt ourselves and judge others.
- Our *apathy* which has hindered us from pursuing relationships with others.
- Our *disunity* which has slowed the work of Christ through his Church and caused his good news to be stifled.

And, realizing that Christ weeps over the cities and came not to "be served, but to serve" (Matthew 20:28), we humbly confess . . .

- Our *unconcern,* manifested by our failure to discover the real needs of our community.
- Our *prayerlessness* for the needs of those around us.
- Our *self-centeredness* that has caused us to care more for ourselves than others.
- Our *selfishness* in not giving the time, resources, and service we ought to the people of Central Arkansas.

OUR COMMITMENT

By the grace of God, and for his glory and the good of others, we commit this day, on the eve of a new millennium . . .

- To *actively promote* unity and fellowship among all true believers in Christ.
- To *vigorously stand* against anything that fosters prejudice or divisiveness.
- To *consistently pray* for the people of Central Arkansas and their leaders.
- To *lovingly serve* the people of these cities through our individual lives, our churches, and our cooperative efforts.

"JUST A BEGINNING"

After ShareFest concluded, we stepped back and tallied the results. The final numbers were impressive:

- Over 100 participating churches
- Over 100 community projects involving more than 3,000 church volunteers
- 1,186 units of blood collected over a three-day period (a regional record) with the American Red Cross
- Two Habitat for Humanity homes built and $80,000 collected to pay for them

- 20,000 meals donated to feed the hungry
- 2,410 children's coats collected
- 4,067 new toys collected for needy children
- 1,002 organ donor cards signed
- $232,000 collected in the love offering at Alltel Arena

The day after ShareFest concluded, the love offering was divided among four local social service agencies. At a press conference, I personally had the joy of presenting each agency director with a check for $58,000.

Harold Nash of the STEP Ministry of North Little Rock was grinning from ear to ear when he said his organization would use the money to expand its tutorial program.

Pat Blackstone, director of Dorcas House, a center for abused women, said their part would go to revamping a child development center.

Al McClendon, director of the North Little Rock Boys and Girls Club, said the club's newfound funds would go toward buying two fourteen-passenger vans to transport children. He said employees have been using their personal vehicles until now.

Positive Atmosphere Reaches Kids (PARK) president, Keith Jackson, former all-pro tight end for the Green Bay Packers, said he planned to use the donation to help pay off the $80,000 mortgage on his group's building. "What an unbelievable gift," he said.

The real gift, however, was not what our churches gave away but what we, the church of Jesus Christ, experienced. We saw God work through us in a powerful, new way. We experienced a new and positive connection with our community and a new sense about ourselves. We established, if only for a moment, a new credibility simply by serving our community *together*. Against love, Paul says, "there is no law" (Galatians 5:22–23).

In his closing comments to those gathered at Alltel Arena, Governor Huckabee had it right. "ShareFest," he said, "is just a beginning. A beginning not just in the sense of repeating an event,

The real gift was not what our churches gave away, but what we, the church of Jesus Christ, experienced . . . a new and positive connection with our community and a new sense about ourselves.

but we pray a beginning of a lifestyle for churches and individual believers who will decide that God has put us on this planet not to be served, but serve." Without this new lifestyle, any attempt at reaching a city for Christ will fail.

Our weary, troubled, and confused world hungers for us, the church, to give them proof. And if we do, they will give our God the glory. I experienced that firsthand during ShareFest. The director of public relations for the American Red Cross approached me to tell me how excited everyone at her agency was at the church's efforts of coming together to give blood. "We cannot believe how much you all are doing," she said. "This is incredible!"

She then went on to tell me that they had made us a special "thank you" card that they all signed in order to show their appreciation. "We really wanted to put a Bible verse on the card that had something to do with blood, but nothing we found seemed appropriate."

I laughed.

"But I did find a perfect verse," she said. "Come and see." As we walked into the lobby to see the giant "thank-you" card the Red Cross had erected there, she told me she had come across this verse quite by accident. "When I read it," she said, "I knew this was it." We were now standing in front of the card prominently displayed for all to see. As I scanned the card a holy shiver went up my spine. Of all the verses this woman could have picked, the one she felt so perfectly summed up her feelings for us and for what we were doing was Matthew 5:16: "Let your light shine before men that they may see your good deeds and praise your Father in heaven."

A sign? Divine coincidence? Maybe. Or perhaps it was simply good old i² feedback on the credibility that's unleashed in the community when churches step above their isolation, competition, and pursuit of reputation for something much more holy: sharing the goodness of Jesus Christ by doing good *together*.

A P.S. . . .

As I have been finishing the final edits on this manuscript, a second ShareFest has just been completed. Again, over one hundred churches participated, mobilizing some 4,300 church volunteers to bless central Arkansas. Working this time in partnership with forty-five corporate sponsors, the effort of this second ShareFest was much more focused and substantial. The needs of central Arkansas public schools were particularly targeted.

The results?

More and better! Rather than elaborate, I'll let the numbers speak for themselves:

- 26 central Arkansas public schools were renovated and refurbished.
- $400,000 of manpower and materials were invested in area schools.
- $21,000 was given for school uniforms for needy children in the three central Arkansas school districts.
- 8,000 Christians gathered in Alltel Arena to pray for our central Arkansas principals, teachers, and students.
- $60,000 was given to Shepherd's Ranch, a faith-based organization aimed at troubled teens.
- $60,000 was given to Black Community Developers, an inner-city agency with programs for at-risk youth.
- $60,000 was given to Joseph Pfeifer Camp, which serves disadvantaged youth in central Arkansas.
- $20,000 was given to the Pulaski County "Our Club" program, an outreach to inner-city gang members.
- $20,000 was given to Friendly Chapel, a ministry that serves the inner city of North Little Rock.
- 21,000 meals were collected for the hungry of central Arkansas.
- 900 units of blood were collected for the American Red Cross.
- 1,500 coats for kids were collected in partnership with the Salvation Army.
- 3,116 new toys were collected for needy children in partership with the Marine Corps Reserves.
- 350 cases of school supplies were collected for needy public school students.

More and better. And to God be the glory!

BRIDGE BUILDER QUESTIONS

Does your church have a vision for the city or just itself? What evidence can you give?

Could you envision a ShareFest-like event happening in your community?

Could you benefit from a prayer movement among pastors like the one described in this chapter? Would you be willing to contact International Renewal Ministry for help?

CHAPTER 10

EQUIPPING LEADERS

Unless we can prepare and release true leaders
to direct our path . . . the church has little
immediate future in America.

—**George Barna,** *The Second Coming of the Church*

A BRIDGE STORY

In 1835 the Rensselaer School was authorized by the state of New York to give instructions in engineering and technology and to offer the new degree of civil engineering. It was the first to do so in the United States and Britain.

One of the school's first renowned alumni was Washington Roebling, who along with his father, John, would go on to build the Brooklyn Bridge. At Rensselaer, Roebling endured more than one hundred different courses, which included Calculus of Variations, Qualitative and Quantitative Analysis, Determinative Mineralogy, Higher Geodesy, Orthographic and Spherical Projections, Acoustics, Optics, Thermotics, Geology of Mining, Paleontology, Rational Mechanics of Solids and Fluids, Spherical Astronomy, Kinematics, and Intellectual and Ethical Philosophy.

A century later, a noted bridge builder and professor of engineering would say of young Roebling's education: "Under such a curriculum, the average college boy of today would be left reeling and staggering. Only the ablest and most ambitious could stand the pace and survive the ordeal."[1] Of the sixty-five students who started out with him, Roebling was only one of twelve to graduate. During his time at Rensselaer, one student committed suicide under the strain.

Years later, Roebling was to take a dim view of such a disconnected education. He said that he saw no point in that terrible treadmill of forcing an avalanche of figures and facts into young brains not qualified to assimilate them yet. Well into a storied career, he would go on to say that he was "still trying to forget the heterogeneous mass of unusable knowledge that I could only memorize, not really digest."[2]

Roebling's criticisms were not stoked on the fires of anti-intellectualism. By nearly everyone's account, he was a bright man. Rather, Roebling instinctively knew what history had already taught: great engineers, more than anything else, were great leaders; and leadership was more about a gathering of wisdom than a collection of facts.

UNTIL NOW, OUR FOCUS has been principally on the bridge-building process itself. By examining that great and awful divide that exists today between churches and their local communities, I have sought to address this modern-day dilemma philosophically, practically, and personally. I have also offered what I believe is the much-needed solution: church bridges of irresistible influence.

Unless the church rediscovers its primary role as bridge builder, the incarnational power of the gospel will remain hidden, and the credibility necessary to reach a culture of cynical, experiential, and spiritually hungry souls will be lost. Even worse, the church's incomparable message of eternal and abundant life, despite relentless weekly proclamation, will continue to be largely ignored. People will simply no longer listen to or attend churches that seem incapable of living out what is preached. Bridges of influence—tangible and evident through the lifestyles and good works of believers—are the only answer.

But such bridges cannot be built without *leaders*. Progressive leaders. Select individuals whose vision extends beyond that of an inwardly "successful church." A "bridge builder" has a vision to raise the lifestyle standards of his people and move his church off its island setting into a city or community. He crafts strategy, builds structure, and measures success, not in terms of size or programming, but in terms of authentic witness, influence, and impact in the community at large. He instinctively knows that "a church's health is measured by its sending capacity, not its seating capacity."[3]

There is no *one* way to find or develop leaders like this, but the need is nothing short of urgent. Everywhere the church is suffering because of a dearth of competent leaders, especially the kind of leader needed to turn the church outward. George Barna has spotlighted this leadership vacuum more vigorously than most. Stating that "only 5 percent of senior pastors say they have the gift of leadership,"[4] he writes: "The church is paralyzed by the absence of godly leadership."[5]

In times of rapid or significant change—and ours is a time of both—success is most likely to be achieved when a strong leader continually reinforces a genuine and powerful vision.

The future of the church largely depends on the emergence of leaders.[6]

Some, of course, would charge that what Barna and others are actually fostering is a fundamental change in what is meant by "pastor." Do we need pastors as CEOs or as shepherds? I believe the scriptural answer is that we need *both:* those who are able shepherds who can teach and exhort (1 Peter 5:2–3), and those who are visionary leaders who can inspire, direct, organize, and innovate (Hebrews 13:7, 17; Romans 12:8). And whereas the facts today point to an abundance of the former, we clearly lack the latter. The church of the twenty-first century is in critical need of pastoral leaders.

NO GREATER INVESTMENT

Recently a board member from another church came to see me. He was concerned that—in his words—"my church is dying." What had once been a large, vibrant body had "dwindled to a few hundred members." For more than an hour, he questioned me about the kinds of innovations and programs we seem to be successfully employing to draw so many people. And then he asked me, "Robert, what should we do?"

Everywhere the church is suffering from a dearth of competent leaders, especially the kind of leader needed to turn the church outward.

It was a question I have had much time to ponder as a pastor at Fellowship Bible Church. Over the last fifteen years we have heavily invested ourselves in planting new churches. In addition, we have regularly consulted with numerous churches from across the United States who have sought us out for advice and support. I have watched with interest as people have aggressively borrowed the blueprints and methodologies of successful churches for the purpose of transplanting them into their own particular settings.

What I have learned from all my firsthand experiences and observations is this: Good ideas, by themselves, are of little worth. In fact, borrowed ideas often do more harm in a church than good, creating dissension and division. In nearly every case, these good ideas lack the mobilizing energy, motivating power, and unifying impact of a leader.

In his book, *The Purpose-Driven Church,* Rick Warren writes, "The most critical factor in a ministry isn't the idea, but the leadership. Each ministry rises or falls on the leadership. Without the right leader, a ministry will just stumble along."[7] "Leaders," Bill Hull observes, "make or break any plan, program, or attempt to renew a congregation."[8]

Without a leader and the unifying and inspirational competencies that leader brings to a given situation, a church that sincerely desires to reinvent itself is in trouble from the start. Without a leader, good ideas mysteriously transform themselves into bad realities. Even though some 500 billion dollars has been spent on church growth materials and seminars during the last fifteen years, the percentage of evangelicals in this country is actually smaller now than before.[9]

It's not that good ideas and new innovations don't matter. . . . It's just that good leaders matter more.

It's not that good ideas and new innovations don't matter. They do. It's just that good leaders matter *more.* And good leaders, not good ideas, are what are so obviously missing in today's evangelical church. Every church, church pastor, and church board should be alarmed at this present deficit of leadership talent.

For the sake of the future, we should be looking within the ranks of our congregations for those young leaders who show even the slightest interest in full-time church ministry. Those who do should be encouraged and helped by the church to go forward in that pastoral interest. Every effort should be made to give them the very best of exposure and opportunity.

Why? Because there is no greater investment in the future of the church than by identifying, encouraging, and providing training for the young leaders in our midst.

It's something every church can do!

There is no greater investment in the future of the church than by identifying, encouraging, and providing training for young leaders in our midst. It's something every church can do!

If you have young, spiritually minded leaders in your church body, then by all means, do whatever it takes to get them the very best training and exposure available. If you are a pastor, spend time with them, take them to today's best churches and church seminars, let them sit with your elder or deacon board, invest financially in their theological training, connect them to the best resources or persons that will enhance their skills, and of course, pray for them.

What if every church did that? What if every church launched one or two of its best and brightest young leaders into kingdom work? Think of the spiritual influence that would unleash!

All of which brings me back to the question my visitor asked me concerning his failing church, "Robert, what should we do?" Even with the present lack of leadership within the church today, my advice was— and still is—simple: "Find a young man with a history and track record of leadership. Not a 'hope-to-be' leader, not a 'want-to-be' leader—a *proven* leader!" This is the most strategic move a church in transition can make. Pray for him, search for him, wait for him. But, don't move until you have him. Good churches and godly leaders go hand in hand. You can't—and you won't—have one without the other.

FINDING AND TRAINING TOMORROW'S LEADERS

Fellowship Bible Church has decided to follow that same advice in taking i² to other communities. We firmly believe that the church as a body of believers has been, is, and will always be, front and center in God's redemptive effort to the world. But for the church to rise above a "spiritual maintenance" mentality or be more than a club or spiritual retreat center, the *right kind* of leader must be found first. This leadership quest, unfortunately, has proven to be more and more difficult. Why? Those leaders just aren't readily available.

As much as I believe in and strongly advocate a rigorous theological education, I also believe young leaders need something more—they need leadership training and mentoring in the field!

Imagine how much better off the evangelical church would be now if half the money spent on church growth seminars had been channeled into the development of leadership. George Barna is absolutely right when he says, "We must commit ourselves to the process of leadership development so that we can empower leaders to succeed." We must not only find these leaders; we must "set them up for success."[10]

So, how do you do that? First off, I believe it will take something more than seminary training. As much as I believe in and strongly advocate a rigorous theological education, I also believe young leaders need something more—*they need leadership training and mentoring in the field!* Like bridge builder Washington Roebling discovered, leadership is more about a gathering of wisdom than a collection of facts. That happens only in a "hands-on" environment, by rubbing up against proven leaders who are interested in their development.

In the early 1990s, as we sought to assist churches seeking our help, we increasingly found ourselves being asked to help them find leaders, and then, after they were hired, to train, mentor, and consult with them. In time, however, those increasing requests and our own growing church created an intolerable situation. We, as staff, simply were being stretched too thin. And yet the opportunity to influence kingdom work beyond our own community was just too important to give up.

Early in 1998, along with several other pastors from Fellowship Bible Church, I attended a small conference in Atlanta. Leadership Network, which sponsored the conference, had invited eleven churches that they had identified as having the potential to effectively train and influence other churches and their leaders. The question on the table was how to best go about such an important and intimidating task.

As we listened and participated in the discussions, it soon became clear—and quite frankly, liberating—that a church staff *could not* pastor and equip their own church while working double-time to help other church leaders succeed. It was just too much.

Several of the churches in attendance had tried to make this arrangement work, much to their regret. In the end, they had burned out staff and suffered, in some instances, serious setbacks in the process. We all could easily identify. During our conversation, a better solution emerged: create a separate organization with "specialty staff," whose focus and mission was exclusively that of training young leaders to plant new churches or empower existing ones.

It was a simple solution. But it had its own challenges too. Where would the money come from to hire these additional staff? Where would these specialists come from? How would they interrelate with the church staff? How would our church react to this new direction?

At Fellowship Bible Church we were determined to find a way. The key motivation, of course, was the idea of influence. Community-impacting influence. We did not want to simply clone ourselves but to influence other churches to grow uniquely. We wanted to influence young leaders and receptive churches to build bridges of irresistible influence to their world—to catch the God-fever of Matthew 5:16.

"DANGEROUS" DREAMS

On paper, still dreaming, we drafted a "company" of staff that could help us accomplish the following objectives:

- Implement a one-year leadership residency program where young seminary leaders could come to Little Rock and gain personal insights and practical skills for implementing a future i2 ministry;
- Strategically plant churches and revitalize others through a leadership network;
- Develop a church consultation wing to respond to specific and ongoing requests for help;
- Create a national church conference to influence churches broadly and help identify potential partnerships.

Our "company," we concluded, would need at least eight full-time staff to be effective. During the next fifteen years—the time at which we predict our church will transition from its existing leadership to a new generation—we would want this team to accomplish the following results:

- Directly plant 100 churches with visionary leaders who will embrace the i2 philosophy;
- Directly influence 1,000 church leaders who would join with us in the pursuit of building bridges of irresistible influence to the community;
- Generally influence 10,000 churches (mainly through our church conferences).

Dangerous dreams? Of course. And, without the intervention of God, just that: dreams. Yet by faith, we decided to pursue the God who is "a rewarder of those who seek Him" (Hebrews 11:6 NASB). We believed then, and still do now, that he gave us these dreams. And we are convinced that, in order to be a catalyst to building bridges of influence beyond our own locale, our focus must be to inspire, encourage, and empower young leaders to become great bridge builders.

So what kind of church leader would we be seeking to influence? Those who possess the following characteristics:

- Keen intellect
- High energy
- A track record of leadership accomplishments
- Spiritual passion and a godly lifestyle
- An ability to think conceptually
- Results-oriented
- An ability to work in a team environment
- A bent toward idealism

Idealism is perhaps *the* critical trait. Great leaders must be willing to recapture, in faith, the Big Idea of Jesus for the church, to persevere against the inevitable hardships, and to work such an idea all the way to its reality. They must be able to actually build tangible bridges, with love, from the church to the world, across seemingly impossible distances.

In the history of bridge building, greatness always directly corresponded to the size of the dream. As engineer Joseph Strauss said on the inauguration of his most daring work, "The Golden Gate Bridge, the bridge that could not and should not be built . . . stands before you in all its majestic splendor." If God so willed, we would seek out leaders who believe the church can be an irresistible influence.

FELLOWSHIP ASSOCIATES

In the winter of 1998, just ten months after we first imagined our "company" on paper, a miracle occurred. Hearing of our dreams, a couple from our church stepped forward to help. Looking back now, it is easy to believe God had sovereignly positioned both them and us for this moment. With hearts desiring to advance God's kingdom and with the unique financial means to do so, this couple graciously offered to underwrite our dreams for five years. Everything!

Within two months what had often been referred to only as the "company" took an official name: "Fellowship Associates." Office space was secured; a young lawyer, Steve Snider, was hired as the new CEO; and an operations team was set up.

So where are we now? As I write this, our dreams are becoming realities. Three seminaries are partnering with us in our leadership residency program. We have just completed our first year of having our first residents on campus. They have experienced first-rate leadership training with both church and business leaders. They have participated weekly with our elder board and church management team, taken MBA classes over the internet, assisted in a number of new ministry ventures, been part of our long-range strategic planning process, and enjoyed regular times of mentoring with our senior staff. Soon a new group will be joining us as residents as we launch those leaving us into new churches. Our goal each year is to prepare these young residents for the leadership responsibilities they will assume in a church, the skills they will need, the challenges they will face, and the pressures they will be under. Specifically, Fellowship Associates hopes to assist them in gaining:

- A greater understanding of the Big Idea of Jesus: the centrality of the vision of building bridges of influence from the church to the world;
- An intimate exposure to successful leaders and proven leadership skills: vision casting, delegation, change management, teamwork, conflict resolution, long-range planning, consensus building, community strategy, etc.;
- An accurate, personal assessment of one's gifts, abilities, and capacities so as to discern the type of environment and team that will be a future "best fit";
- A deeper commitment to personal holiness and spiritual dependence;
- A plan for ongoing personal development and marriage and family enrichment.

As well as we are able, we want to set these gifted individuals up for success—not only in the training we give, but also in the ongoing personal support we intend to offer after they have left us for the churches they will lead.

But there is more happening than just our residency program. Fellowship Associates also enables us to respond more effectively to churches and church leaders seeking us out for assistance, resourcing, and consulting. Though we will stay selective, the staff of Fellowship Associates enables us to better serve those church leaders with whom we have and will have partnerships and alliances.

Finally, through Fellowship Associates we are now able to offer and to host an annual national church training conference. Our aim here is to share the best of what we know with as many churches as possible. More information about any of these—our leadership residency program, our resources, or our annual church training conference, can be obtained at www.fellowshipassociates.com.

Of course, in all our efforts, we are anchored in great humility. We are aware that pride, in so many ways and in so many forms, can come slipping under the door. We do not believe even for a moment that we are God's solution to the problems facing the contemporary church. What we hope with all our hearts is that we can, in some way, be a positive influence. We feel we have a responsibility—a mandate—to share what we have learned, mostly by trial and error, with those who have the greatest potential for influence: leaders.

> *Every church can and should be encouraging its brightest and best to consider leadership in God's church.*

In my opinion, leadership is far and away the single greatest need of the church entering the twenty-first century. We need leaders! And we need to be crying out to God to give us leaders. It should be at the top of every evangelical church's prayer list. Without them, any hope for church renewal is mere fantasy.

I am aware that few churches will have the resources and opportunity to train leaders in the same fashion as Fellowship Bible Church has. But surely many churches are able to invest a portion of their budgets and staff time into equipping at least one prequalified seminary graduate per year in the basics of church leadership. Imagine the impact over ten, twenty, and thirty years! And every church *can* and should be encouraging its brightest and best to consider leadership in God's church. Imagine what would happen if every church "harvested" just one leader for the kingdom!

So in every church, regardless of size or resources, there are two very practical ways to build a bridge of irresistible influence, two ways to connect the church effectively to the community, two ways to be salt and light. One way is by equipping your congregation to directly influence your community through the lifestyles they pursue and the good works they effectively initiate. Such a path requires courageous vision, much teaching and exhortation, and meaningful practical applications.

The other way to irresistible influence is by developing the life and leadership skills of a young bridge builder. I believe they are out there: select individuals who can lead tomorrow's church and spiritually influence the community too. What's needed is for every church to find them, challenge them, invest in them, train them (or find training for them), and call them to lead the church out of its present-day wilderness to holy ground. i².

Despite all that today's church is consumed with (or consumed by), finding and training young godly leaders is of supreme importance.

The future of the evangelical church rests in how well we do.

BRIDGE BUILDER QUESTIONS

Does your church have a way of identifying future church leaders within your congregation and encouraging them? How?

What support—financial, personal, practical—could a young leader interested in the ministry expect from your church? Is the development of future church leaders a priority of your present church leadership?

CHAPTER 11

DEVELOPING A COMMUNITY STRATEGY

If you are serious about having your church make an impact,

become an expert in your community. Pastors should know

more about their communities than anyone else.

—**Rick Warren,** *The Purpose-Driven Church*

A BRIDGE STORY

In "Bridges," Judith Dupree writes of one of the world's most compelling bridges:

The Erasmus Bridge, Ben van Berkel's glorious arching portal over the Maas River, operates as a vital connector between the two halves of the Dutch city of Rotterdam—the civic institutions on the river's north bank and the ambitious urban regeneration scheme known as the Kop van Zuid to the south. Its robust, asymmetrical form is actually three bridges in one. The combination—a cable-stayed bridge with a main span of 918 feet, a side span viaduct, and a bascule bridge—indicates the multitude of urban, technical, and design considerations that figured in its construction.

Rotterdam, left a blank slate by World War II, has determinedly rebuilt itself, powered by a plan devised in 1946 for the reconstruction of the inner city. Contemporary architecture, high-rise buildings, wide boulevards, and the pioneering reuse of old harbor basins and quays are hallmarks of the city today. Since its opening, the Erasmus Bridge has presided over Rotterdam's energetic transformation.[1]

There is a complex relationship between a great bridge and the city in which it resides. Research, understanding, and reflection must precede the work of construction. The engineer's greatest pursuit is not so much in making a bridge stand as in making it "a fit"; that is, making it an integral, complementing, and deepening reality within the community it serves. Bridges, as works of art, do not simply function; they are sensitive, well-conceived, and well-thought-out catalysts of change unique to each community.

For the engineer, this is not simple work. It demands a working knowledge, beyond the laws of physics and structural designs, into the much more elusive comprehension of the soul and spirit of a community, into what it "really needs." In the triangle of architecture, artistry, and community understanding, a great bridge, in a sense, connects with the city before it seeks to change it.

AS YEARS GO, 1957 had more than its share of dramatic, life-changing events. It was the year Pan American Airways inaugurated the first American jet service to Europe, opening one of the many supersonic bridges between continents that were to come and constructing what was heretofore unthinkable: a global village. Ford Motor Company unveiled a new, sexy car called the "Thunderbird" at the International Automobile Show, which status-hungry Americans would lust over for years to come. Our nation's first atomic power plant went on-line, generating electricity in Pennsylvania with the lofty expectation of cheap, clean, and perhaps unlimited energy for the future. And the relatively new medium of television allowed the nation to watch its first NFL championship game ever, *live*.

But 1957 is also special for another reason. It was the year fourteen-year-old Elizabeth Eckford took the longest walk of her life. And it turned her world and the city in which I live upside down.

Elizabeth would later be known as one of the "Little Rock Nine," a group of black students called on to integrate Little Rock's Central High School. On September 4, 1957, however, she was all alone. Separated by a twist of fate from her companions, she found herself walking through a gauntlet of jeering white people to the front doors of the now-famous high school. It became a defining moment.

As this courageous journey played out before photographers and cameras, the pictures and stories of her lonely ordeal became national news within hours. Later, Elizabeth would recollect her harrowing memories:

> Before I left home, Mother called us into the living room. She said we should have a word of prayer. Then I caught the bus and got off a block from the school. I wondered whether I could make it to the center entrance a block away. It was the longest block I ever walked in my whole life. Even so, I still wasn't too scared, because all the time I was thinking the guards [the National Guard soldiers called in by Governor Faubus to keep order] would protect me. . . .
>
> I stood looking at the school—It looked so big! Just then, the guards let some white students go through. . . . When I was able to steady my knees, I walked up to the guard who had let the

white students in. He didn't move. When I tried to squeeze past him, he raised his bayonet, and then the other guards closed in and they raised their bayonets. They moved closer and closer. Somebody started yelling, "Lynch her! Lynch her!" I tried to see a friendly face somewhere in the mob—someone who maybe would help. I looked into the face of an old woman and it seemed a kind face, but when I looked at her again, she spat on me.[2]

Elizabeth Eckford survived. In fact, she became a national hero of civil rights. But the awful ordeal and the tragic events surrounding the Central High crisis did more than break one link in the chain of Southern segregation. It also dramatically shaped the story of the central Arkansas community in which I live. Even as I write, more than forty-three years later, the events of 1957 still powerfully influence the personality, perspectives, and social issues of Little Rock and our across-the-river neighbor, North Little Rock.

Every community has a story. A unique story. Every community has a character, a "feel," and an attitude shaped by its own peculiar events and circumstances. And that particular context must be thoroughly understood and considered by any church wanting to make an impact on its community in a meaningful way. Without such understanding, we will put forth a guesswork kind of effort. Or, to use a Pauline phrase, we "beat the air," but without aim (1 Corinthians 9:26).

Every community has a story. . . . And that particular context must be thoroughly understood and considered by any church wanting to make an impact on its community in a meaningful way.

When it comes to building a bridge of meaningful spiritual influence to a community, our first act must be to ask, "What's the story here? What's really going on? What are the real issues, the real problems, the real needs?" *Believe it or not, rarely if ever does a church do this.* Our usual mode of operation is to act without asking and minister in a context void of facts and objective understanding. Jack Dennison is right when he says, "If we are to succeed in our mission to further God's kingdom on earth, we must gather information that allows us to see our communities as they really are, and not merely as they appear to be."[3] Proverbs 18:13 puts it more bluntly: "He who answers before listening—that is his folly and his shame."

Only when we have real, objective answers about our community can a ministry strategy begin to emerge that wisely and effectively connects the church to the city. Michael Regele says, "Pastors don't need to become experts in sociology and anthropology; what they need to do is develop the skills of walking into a community setting . . . and analyzing that setting to figure out what is going on there. Contextual analysis includes demographics, understanding the power structures of a community, understanding the economic base, and understanding what gives the particular ethos of that community."[4]

SEEKING A REALISTIC PICTURE

The need to know a more detailed story of our community has become increasingly important to our church in light of our i² vision. Every spring, as we graduate church members from their Season of Life growth groups into their new Common Cause service groups, the question of "What does our community really need?" has grown louder and louder.

You would think we would have answered that question at the beginning, when our new i² ministry structure was first put in place. But I must confess that something this obvious often gets overlooked. We were so busy rallying our people to creatively use their gifts and serve that we somehow neglected addressing where that service was most needed in our particular community context.

The need for objective data and "contextual analysis" only increased with each new spring graduation. As we formed Common Cause groups, we intended to be more than just busy. We hungered to be strategic!

Several of the pastors I had been working with in the city suggested a formal research survey as a way to gain the understanding we now knew we desperately needed.

In biblical history, taking a survey before acting is not unique. Moses and Joshua certainly conducted them when they sent spies into the Promised Land. Wisely, they sought a realistic picture of the obstacles, challenges, and rewards ahead of them before determining how to move forward. Nehemiah, too, was a surveyor. Before investing himself in the reconstructing of the city of Jerusalem, he spent days assessing the situation through firsthand inspections (Nehemiah 2). Only then did he seek to formulate a plan.

In seeking to build bridges of spiritual influence to our city, we had gotten the process backward. We were drawing up plans based on *our* interests and *our* instincts, and launching ministries on guesswork without first grounding them in research—the facts. It was time to change that.

From the first moment a survey was mentioned to our church, good things began to happen. First, the elders of Fellowship Bible Church agreed that our church should underwrite the project financially. Qualified people then came forward and offered their help. Don Hinman, who has a doctorate in research design and is an executive for a major information management company, offered to head up the survey's design. Alan Bell, a business consultant, and John Earl, a member with public relations expertise, also came on board. These men, along with church staff members Ray Williams, Paul Stevens, Jerry Richardson, and Mel Petty, were charged by the elders to create an overall survey design and then submit it to a number of independent market research firms that might be interested in bidding on the project.

After a number of team meetings and hours of discussion, we agreed to a three-phase survey design.

Phase One: Community Research

The plan here was to review and summarize research previously conducted on the needs of our community during the last ten years. We discovered such research was abundant (any local research firm can direct you to where such information is available). But much to our surprise, it had never been analyzed *together*. Therefore, phase one was organized to take the best of the needs assessment work already done in central Arkansas (fifteen excellent studies were eventually evaluated in detail) and from them, establish a well-documented and highly defensible list of the *real needs* of our community.

Phase Two: Focus Group Feedback

This phase was to consist of two separate focus groups composed of twenty-two community and social service leaders representing major components within our city (political, educational, business, non-profits, etc.). The focus group participants would be provided the list of "real needs" uncovered from the phase one research and then asked to interact with the findings. Focus group participants would also be asked how they would personally prioritize the needs of our community and what needs they would suggest the church community give primary attention to.

Phase Three: Survey of Churches

Surveys would be mailed to each of the 633 churches that comprise the central Arkansas area. The survey would request membership demographics, facility data, and most important, detailed information concerning the kinds of ministry programs each church offers to its members and the community. By comparing the ministry information of all the churches with the needs list gathered in phase one, some objective assessment could be made as to how connected or disconnected the central Arkansas churches are to the real needs of our community.

After completing the project design, our survey team entertained proposals from various research companies interested in conducting our survey. Of course, by hiring a respected research firm, our survey would be seen by the community not only as professionally credible but also as objective. The firm Market Insights was eventually chosen. Several months of collaboration with Market Insights followed, and then the survey commenced. Six months later, it was finished.

SOME SURPRISING RESULTS

So what did we learn? For the first time, I can look at my community in a way I never could before—*with the facts*. And while the survey provided all kinds of insights and helpful bits of information, five facts stood out:

FACT #1: *The popular perception that central Arkansas is a highly "churched" community is wrong.*

Because Little Rock is part of the Bible Belt, with churches visible everywhere, it is easy to assume we are a strong, churchgoing community. Certainly, that has been the general perception. But the facts uncovered by our survey proved otherwise.

> *Because Little Rock is part of the Bible Belt, with churches visible everywhere, it is easy to assume we are a strong, church-going community.... But the facts uncovered by our survey proved otherwise.*

The population of Little Rock and North Little Rock together is approximately 350,000. With 633 identified churches in our community, the research estimates church attendance in central Arkansas somewhere between 30 and 40 percent. In comparison, the national average for church attendance is 40 percent. So instead of being "highly churched," we are, at best, only average. And some of our research suggests that we are much lower than that, somewhere in the 25 to 30 percent range.

Research like this, by the way, can also bring good news to a city. When I lived in Portland, Oregon, attending seminary, I was told over and over how unchurched that city was. The prevailing belief was that the size of the church community there was somewhere between 3 and 9 percent of the population of 1.75 million. But when survey research was completed on Portland, the Christian population was found to be much larger. Jack Dennison writes, "The average worship attendance of the church in Portland was actually 350,000, or 20 percent of the population! When you add the 20 percent or so who are regular attenders but absent on any given Sunday, this puts the worshipping community at 420,000—about one in every four persons in the city."[5]

The point is, when it comes to the church in a community, looks can be deceiving. Things are not necessarily as they appear to be. And for us in central Arkansas, the assumption that "most everyone goes to a church" is an illusion.

FACT #2: *Race and education are still dominant issues in our community.*

The research showed that the problems that exploded in public in 1957 are still just as prominent today. This was especially evident through the comments of community leaders who served as focus group participants. They ranked race and education at the top as the two most critical issues of our community.

Particularly troublesome in the focus groups was the fact that, in regard to race and education, many saw the church as a negative contributor. Said one, "Sunday is still the most segregated hour in our city." Others expressed concern over church schools. Several blamed these schools for continuing "white flight," which "has only broadened the chasm between the church and our community." Still another focus group participant put it this way: "If church schools are really about education, then they must give real effort to racial integration, too." Clearly, race and education are huge stumbling blocks in our central Arkansas community.

Particularly troublesome in the focus groups was the fact that, in regard to race and education, many saw the church as a negative contributor.

But they are not the only issues.

In addition to race and education, our phase one community research survey that analyzed and summarized fifteen studies on the needs of our community also documented eight other major issues impacting our area. They were:

- Affordable housing
- Domestic violence
- Health-care access
- Youth in poverty
- Substance abuse
- Elderly issues
- Transportation
- Economics/Employment

So what help does rich data like this give to the churches of central Arkansas? First, it helps the church to know where the real needs of the commnity are without further guesswork. Second, it offers up these key needs as prime targets for ministry investment when a church becomes serious about bridging the community. Third, it begs a biblical question: "Am I my brothers' keeper?" At Fellowship Bible Church, we can use this list to imagine all kinds of future Common Cause ministries.

But regardless of what the church does, the facts are in. And these ten issues *are* the major needs of central Arkansas.

FACT #3: *There is presently a wide gap between the major needs of the community and the availability of programs in churches to meet those needs.*

The survey demonstrated that community needs and church ministry programs miss each other like proverbial ships in the night. Only three of the community's ten major needs identified by the survey are currently being addressed by area churches in any significant way. They are youth in poverty (youth programs, child-care programs, early childhood development programs, after-school youth programs); substance abuse (Alcoholics Anonymous and other drug and substance abuse programs); and elderly issues (elderly programs). Housing needs and domestic violence also had support from a few local churches, but only in a very limited way.

The survey demonstrated that community needs and church ministry programs miss each other like proverbial ships in the night.

The majority of churches were consumed with traditional programs generally associated with religious institutions: worship services, Sunday school, and spiritual outreach and evangelism. Unfortunately, these do little to connect the church and the community together.

FACT #4: *Central Arkansas churches invest very little money in local ministry programs.*

It was discovered that 18 percent of church budgets are used for ministry programs. However, less than a third of that—a mere 5 percent—is spent locally. That means more money is given to reaching the world than to our own central Arkansas community. And the lack of this community investment by the church, either in terms of money or ministry, shows. Rarely is the church mentioned publicly as being an asset to our area by anyone. We are generally ignored by community leaders and often left out of community life.

Recently the Little Rock Chamber of Commerce published a well-scripted, full-color pamphlet advertising our city. It was a handsome piece, produced for use in recruiting new businesses and industry to our area as well as in welcoming newcomers. Page after page listed the strengths, benefits, and beauty of our community. Every aspect of community life was covered: the River Market district, the arts, parks and recreation, the schools, neighborhood associations, city government, and so forth. Everything was mentioned—*except the church.*

Not one paragraph, picture, or even word was given on the faith community. Zero! When that was pointed out to a Chamber of Commerce official, he was genuinely embarrassed. "That can't be true," he said thumbing back through the brochure. But it was. The fault of that obvious omission, however, did not lie with the Chamber of Commerce. To blame them would surely have been the wrong kind of finger-pointing. No, the omission was clearly self-inflicted; and the church, with facts in hand, has no one to blame but itself.

FACT #5: *The community welcomes church involvement.*

For many churches, this last fact is probably surprising. Rather than being antagonistic to church involvement, our research demonstrated that the community was actually looking to churches for more involvement and wondering why they weren't there. In other words, the lack of bridges between the church and community was due, not to a lack of interest or even desire on the community's part, but to a lack of interest and initiative on the church's part.

Our research demonstrated that the community was actually looking to churches for more involvement and wondering why they weren't there.

Here is an excerpt from the project's findings:

The time is right for faith organizations that want to have a more significant impact on their neighborhood of residence. Several organizations (city, not-for-profit, and university) were interested and open to greater participation by the faith-based community to address needs within neighborhoods.... Churches were perceived [by the community] to be under-utilized resources that offer important possibilities for social and community progress. The visibility of the faith-community generally is not well integrated with other neighborhood groups.

Those words, "not well integrated" and "under-utilized," hurt! But that is how the churches of central Arkansas are perceived by our community.

In the focus groups, a similar openness to church involvement was exposed. The only reservation, noted by several participants, regarded evangelism. One put it this way: "Churches should not try to push their religious views on anyone. But if they would just open their arms to those in need."

One could take offense at a statement like that or see it, as I do, as an opening. The whole premise of this book has been to restore the incarnational aspect of the gospel. Disconnected words, absent a body of works, not only fail to build a bridge but also dig a moat. People today need to *see* the gospel first. If we can deliver it with "open arms"—and our community is asking for it—is there any doubt that evangelism will follow? Will not the gospel of faith flourish in an atmosphere of love and good deeds? Certainly Jesus, the apostles, and the early church thought so.

SURVEY RECOMMENDATIONS

These five facts, along with the rest of the research, provide for the churches of central Arkansas not only an accurate feel for the story of our community but also an understanding of our place and standing in it. It is this understanding that serves as a foundation—a baseline—for assessing our condition and implementing a sound ministry strategy. The research survey itself recommended the following five ministry suggestions for better connecting the church with the community:

SURVEY RECOMMENDATIONS

1. Churches should reassess their ministry programs, giving consideration to the high-priority needs identified by the survey in the community. While not every church will have the resources to develop effective programs in all areas, those need areas a church can touch, it should. Programs which support the family, neighborhoods, and education appear to have the greatest potential to address a variety of needs in a holistic manner.

2. Churches should focus on existing ministries in the community which are already working successfully before starting new ones.
3. Churches should continue to look for strategic ways to work together to serve the community. This would not only offer the opportunity to accomplish things that can only be achieved by united efforts; it would also communicate a positive and refreshing message to the general public.
4. Churches should look for opportunities to partner with other organizations in the community which are both effectively responding to the high priority needs and which are consistent with the church's mission.
5. Building on a common faith in Jesus Christ, churches should be actively pursuing authentic racial reconciliation. Taking this step is critical to the health of our community. Progress here will not come from artificial programming, but will be the result of building relationships and working toward genuine equality in the high-priority areas identified in the research.

So now we know.

We know what the real needs of our community are. We know the major issues and challenges. We know the true condition of the church. We know what it does and doesn't do and why its influence is so small in the central Arkansas community. We also know what we can do to change that. *We know because we have the facts!*

I only wish this research had occurred several years ago, so I could share how responsive the churches have been to this information. We, as pastors, are only now digesting this fresh information. But it is already having an impact.

At our most recent pastors' prayer summit, this information and how we could respond to it was on everyone's lips. Some pastors from predominantly white churches suggested hiring black staff members in the future. "Only then," said one, "will our congregations have any real chance of affecting the racial diversity that exists in our city."

"Yes, and only then will the church take the lead toward true racial reconciliation," said another.

The need to move church ministry into the city was another strong suggestion. Instead of holding quality classes on marriage, parenting, finances, and other life skills inside the church, the research recommended, *"Take them into the community!"* Offer them at noon in the business district, at night in the neighborhood associations, to inner-city churches who often lack these options.

We know what the real needs of our community are. We know the major issues and challenges. We know the true condition of the church.... We know because we have the facts!

Another positive idea was having the Nehemiah Group (the city pastors' leadership team) host an all-church training seminar to teach area churches and pastors ways to adjust their structures and ministries to better connect with the community. Church consultants could be brought in, and churches that are presently having a community impact could be showcased to give our local churches hands-on examples of how to become more community effective.

Finally, it was suggested that church schools aggressively address the issue of education and race. While most church schools were created out of a concern for preserving Christian values and providing quality education, for much of the black community and others, it looks like "just another form of segregation." The only way for that to change is for Christian schools to show that Christian education is for everyone. And to do that, they must actively recruit not only black students, but students from all races. It was suggested at our prayer summit that we as church pastors could actively promote this pursuit. "Our churches should give money to that end," one pastor said. "Provide scholarships."

In light of the facts, what a witness all this would be! What "good news" it would offer to our community from the church of Jesus Christ and what leadership!

Only time will tell.

On September 4, 1957, Elizabeth Eckford prayed with her family and then took the longest walk of her life. It was a strategic and courageous journey that changed the course of a city. My city.

Now it's the church's turn to do the same. In our final chapter, I will spell out the radical steps that need to be taken. So let us pray, swallow hard, take courage, and begin together the long journey back to the communities God has called us to love and redeem.

BRIDGE BUILDER QUESTIONS

What do you know "as fact" about the needs of your community and the condition of the churches in your area?

What would your church do if it had access to the kind of research information I have described in this chapter? Would it make any difference?

Would your church be willing to go in with other churches in the community and hire a research firm to do survey work for you?

PART FIVE

ANTICIPATING THE FUTURE

The Church in the

Twenty-first Century

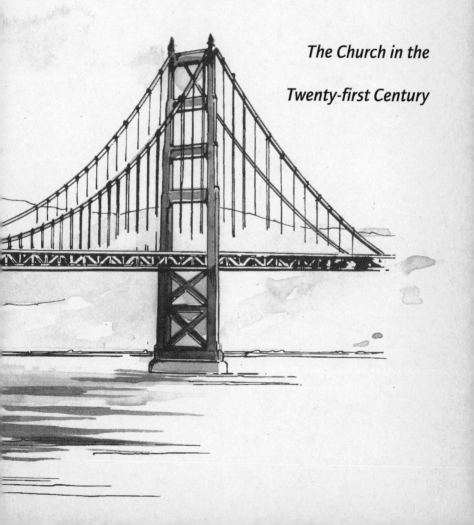

CHAPTER 12

FROM HERE TO WHERE?

People today show interest in the truth of the gospel
only after they've seen the relevance of the church
and the credibility of Christians.

—**Elmer Town and Warren Bird**, *Into the Future*

A Bridge Story

When it came to building the Chunnel connecting England with France, the French had the
perfect word for it: bicephele. Two-headed. There
were two mammoth firms: Eurotunnel, which was
charged with the finance, ownership, and operation
of the Chunnel; and Transmanche-Link, a consor-
tium of contractors responsible for building it. Each
of these two were also two-headed: equally French
and British. Both of the firms were built from
scratch.

No one was ever allowed to take charge. Leadership, more times than not, was reduced to the management of conflict, not progress. Said a
high-ranking executive brought in during a desperate leadership change mandated by the banks, "The
project . . . created a lot of tension because it [was]
not geared to solving problems; it [was] geared to
placing blame. Everybody kept reading the contract
rather than looking for ways to make it work."[1] The

same official gave the successful completion of construction about a 30 percent chance.

The English yelled at the French, and the French yelled at the English. The pressure of time amplified the disagreements: Seven years was allotted for the design, engineering, and construction. Contractually, no consideration was given to cost or time overruns. In the end, that meant a great deal of money was lost.

Said one executive, "There were nervous breakdowns galore."[2]

The problems were primarily centered around a lack of shared standards. The two countries "had a different word for everything."[3] Everything had to be translated. The French had their own accounting system; so did the English. The French ran on 380 volts, and the British on 420. Construction manuals were bilingual. There were even two different standards used to measure sea level. In a literal sense, the English and the French could not figure out where each other were coming from.

"When you have people coming from two different nations," said one of the engineers, "each believes that only their regulations are right."[4]

FOR MOST OF THE twentieth century, the church in the United States has stood as a house divided:

- Liberal versus conservative;
- Openness versus orthodoxy;
- Social justice versus spiritual justification;
- Tolerance versus repentance;
- Inclusiveness versus evangelism;
- Great Commandment versus the Great Commission.

It has been America's version of the Hundred Years' War, and it has left both camps, with their two versions of Christianity, wounded and strategically crippled.

Separately, severed from one another, each side seeks to claim victory. Both have had their brief moments in the sun. Liberals can point to their many social causes, such as their support of the Civil Rights movement in the 1960s. Conservatives, on the other hand, can boast of huge increases in both membership and popularity, which led *Time* magazine to proclaim 1980 "The Year of the Evangelical."

But a house divided cannot stand. Both sides have also suffered greatly. For liberals, social compassion shorn of spiritual truth has led to standing for everything and nothing at the same time. Shrinking budgets, stunning losses in membership, and a growing moral and spiritual confusion are the inevitable results and serve as warning signs of an even greater catastrophe ahead if spiritual compromise continues.

Likewise, evangelical triumphs have been shaded with deadly downsides. Prosperity has given birth to arrogance and extremism, both of which, when disconnected from love, have pierced the mirage of success. The evangelical voice that fervently won so many into an authentic relationship with Jesus Christ also tended to degenerate publicly into a shrill shout: telling Americans how to live, think, and vote. Evangelicals acted as if they possessed an exclusive understanding of what was right and who was right. And predictably, the cultural reaction to this "being talked down to" has been tragic and alienating.

A huge distrust of, and hostility toward, evangelicals has developed, which we on "the right" clearly don't understand and have yet to come to grips with. We are feared, loathed, and disliked. And the more we shout at the world from our pulpits, pews, and studios, the more feared and repulsive we become.

Most of the twentieth century was a story of separation. Of an either/or Christianity. Either a social gospel *or* a spiritual gospel. Either a horizontal construct emphasizing human compassion *or* a vertical construct emphasizing amazing grace.

But isn't the cross a powerful combination of both? The horizontal *and* the vertical? Isn't the cross, in fact, a bridge, uniting supernatural and human realities?

Clearly, that bridge needs to be reconnected in the twenty-first century. But it will surely prove as difficult as connecting, say, England with France. For liberals, that will mean painfully re-embracing orthodoxy. For evangelicals, that will mean humbly reengaging the community and addressing real needs. It can no longer be either/or. Not if the church wants to live and thrive. Not if it wants to reclaim a place of influence. It has to embrace the both/and to once again become the penetrating salt and light that Jesus originally had in mind.

"BUT THEN SOMETHING HAPPENED . . ."

Where did the evangelical church suffer this damaging social disconnect? How did our gospel become so one-sided, offering God's word to the world without the balance of an equal share of good works? Have we always been this way?

British theologian John Stott offers us an enlightening historical perspective. He asserts that evangelicals of the eighteenth and nineteenth centuries were a more unified group than their twentieth-century counterparts, investing themselves vigorously in both evangelism *and* social involvement. In the process, they not only transformed hearts but a good portion of society as well. The works of John and Charles Wesley, William Wilberforce, and Charles Finney are but a few of the many outstanding examples that could be cited.

"But then something happened," Stott writes. "At some point during the first thirty years of the twentieth century, and especially during the decade following World War I, a major shift took place which American historian Timothy L. Smith has termed, 'The Great Reversal.'"[5] Evangelicals disconnected with social action and community

needs. We retreated from the public square. Our churches reduced their mission to saving souls, serving our congregations, and defending the faith. This continues, for the most part, to this day.

Why? Stott lists five specific reasons:

1. *The evangelical reaction against theological liberalism.* At the turn of the century, liberalism was seeping into the churches of Europe and America. Eyeing this threat, evangelicals over-reacted by concentrating solely on vindicating the faith from what they considered monstrous heresy. In the process, they neglected their social responsibility and heritage.

> *At some point during the first thirty years of the twentieth century ... evangelicals disconnected with social action and community needs.*

2. *The division of the gospel into "social" and "spiritual" categories.* The most popular liberal spokesman of the social gospel, Walter Rauschenbush, declared, "It's not a matter of getting individuals into heaven, but of transforming life on earth into the harmony of heaven." In response, evangelicals made "getting into heaven" their chief and sometimes only concern.

3. *Evangelicals' disillusionment with earthly life after World War I.* After this horrible war, man and society appeared beyond reformation. As good as past social efforts had been, what good were they in light of this? Why involve oneself in earthly causes that were sure to fail again and again in the hands of depraved humanity?

4. *The spread of premillennialism.* This popular theological position predicts a steady deterioration of life on earth until the coming of Jesus and his millennial reign. Therefore, many reason, if the world is getting worse and worse and only Jesus at his coming can make it right, what point is there in trying to reform it now? Evangelical leader Ray Stedman once made that exact point when he said, "No matter what the church does as God's instrument in the world, the ultimate end of the world will be anarchy and chaos. . . . No, the church is not here to improve the world."[6]

5. *The spread of evangelical Christianity among the upper and middle classes who equated it, more and more, with their own personal well-being.* Evangelicalism became more and more associated with self-absorbed

individuals preoccupied with finding health and happiness for their own lives and maintaining the status quo in an unstable world. As this concern for the individual increased, concern for society at large correspondingly decreased.[7]

Whether one agrees with any or all of Stott's analysis, the point remains: the evangelical church at the beginning of this century finds itself postured much differently than it was a hundred years ago. Our rich heritage of influencing society through humble acts of charity, strategic community concern, and sacrificial works of service has been largely forsaken and has been replaced by a one-sided gospel of proclamation. As one evangelical pastor recently confessed to me, "This good works stuff in the community is new to me. I'm just not comfortable with it."

> *As people who pride themselves in their loyalty to Scripture, how can we ignore the call to good works in the community that the Bible so emphatically exhorts us to?*

We have focused on the Word to the exclusion of the greater and more powerful reality of "making the Word flesh." In this posture, the evangelical church finds itself, not surprisingly, disconnected from the real world. We are isolated, self-absorbed, and socially uninvolved. In this regard, Jack Dennison warns, "The church of the twenty-first century must shift its focus from an institutional orientation to a community orientation if it is to survive and thrive."[8] As people who pride themselves in their loyalty to Scripture, how can we ignore the call to good works in the community that the Bible so emphatically exhorts us to? Ponder these words by John Stott:

> It is exceedingly strange that any followers of Jesus Christ should ever have needed to ask whether social involvement was their concern, and that controversy should have blown up over the relationships between evangelism and social responsibility. For it is evident that in his public ministry, Jesus both "went about teaching . . . and preaching" (Matthew 4:23; 9:35 RSV) and "went about doing good and healing" (Acts 10:38 RSV). In consequence, evangelism and social concern have been intimately related to one another throughout the history of the church.[9]

Now that the evangelical church has entered a new millennium, it must jettison the either/or construct that has shaped, defined, and plagued us. It is time to re-embrace the both/and that alone gives us a clear strategy of how to build strong churches that serve as bridges of irresistible influence—bridges that are supported by the steel girders of truth *and* proof, proclamation *and* incarnation. Bridges allowing for the transport of common grace to the needy as well as amazing grace to the receptive.

WHAT IF WE CONTINUE BUSINESS AS USUAL?

My fear is that most evangelicals will consider the call as simply too high, the work too great, the climb too steep, the change required too drastic. But if we do go on as we are, soothing our consciences with a contemporary face-lift, we can and must expect a further disintegration, not only in our influence but in two things essential to our future: our *name* and our *perspective*.

The Bible says, "A good name is more desirable than great riches" (Proverbs 22:1). Names are summaries. They come to embody all that is or isn't about a person or group, true or false, real or imagined. They also carry in them the powerful weight of emotion that ignites when a name is mentioned. That's why the Bible, as well as any good marketer, holds up the high value of a name.

Though we might call ourselves Baptist, Assembly of God, Evangelical Free, Bible Church, Presbyterian, Pentecostal, Vineyard, Christian Missionary Alliance, or something else, the more important name is not the one we call ourselves, but the one by which we are called. And by what name does the world call us as evangelicals? One comes immediately to mind: "the Religious Right."

What image does this name bring to mind? What emotions does it evoke? If we are honest, we will admit it is a name associated with nonloving confrontations, judgmental pronouncements, and self-righteous invitations to be more like us. If we are really honest, it could be considered in close company with another name with which we are all too familiar: "Pharisee."

Smug. Right. Rigid. Vocal. Demanding. Uninvolved. The Pharisees were the Religious Right of the first century. As Jesus said, they laid on people heavy loads, but they were "not willing to lift a finger to move them" (Matthew 23:4). They proclaimed righteousness, but inwardly were "full of hypocrisy" (Matthew 23:28) and empty of compassion (as highlighted in the story of the Good Samaritan, Luke 10:31–33).

These are increasingly the feelings our name evokes in American society. Say "evangelical," and words like *condescending, dogmatic, scary, demanding,* and *controlling* scroll across the mind. Images boil to the surface of preachy moral pronouncements, boycotts, picketing, and political pressure—to conform state to church, to make people behave, to make them act more like us, for we are always right.

Is it any great wonder that we find ourselves the object of ridicule or fear? This is a far cry from Matthew 5:16, where Jesus imagined a church of good works that would cause the world to give glory to God.

By contrast, let's look at another name: Mormon. Despite the dark suspicion this religion has often labored under since its beginning over a century ago, Mormonism today is mainstream. It possesses a name no longer locked up in fear, but one interlocked with family, decency, and high standards of clean living.

What caused this change of perception? First, Mormons are strategically engaged with the American culture. Like it or not, they regularly speak to the general public in an area where most Americans are desperate to succeed: the family. Rather than relentlessly decrying the world's ills, they are powerfully conversing with its needs. They offer help and resources, not for a contribution, but for free. A good deal of it may be media-driven through slick, professionally produced TV spots, but it's nonetheless friendly, effective, and always done with excellence.

Second, Mormons display a unique lifestyle that offers a measure of convincing proof. For example, sending their sons in white shirts and ties around the world for two years of mission work is a powerful picture worth more than a thousand words. It shows real conviction to a world craving sight. All this makes for good press and, in time, builds a good reputation. Clearly, we could learn a thing or two.

The strategic way Mormons have engaged the world certainly hasn't hurt their effectiveness either. Mormonism is now one of America's two fastest growing religions (Islam being the other).[10] A good name is a powerful asset. It immediately connects us to the world.

But a name is not the only thing in jeopardy with evangelicals. Of even greater concern is the state of our *perspective,* or as the *American Dictionary* explains it, our "ability to perceive things in their actual interrelations." Do evangelical Christians today perceive the church's relationship to the world correctly? Increasingly, the feedback seems to offer an emphatic *No.* Even as society embraces spirituality and as the supernatural becomes chic, evangelicalism seems awkwardly out of step: our influence waning, our growth stagnant, our image questionable, our name invalidated. As Jack Dennison writes, "Church growth specialists have placed the percentage of unhealthy congregations in the United States as between 70–80 . . . such congregations have little, if any, sense of the needs and opportunities of their community and have lost sight of their reason for existing."[11]

> **D**o evangelical Christians today perceive the church's relationship to the world correctly? Increasingly, the feedback seems to offer an emphatic No.

THREE i² REQUIREMENTS

So what do we do? That, of course, depends on our ability to perceive things in their actual interrelations. If we perceive all this through self-righteous eyes, we will no doubt choose to vindicate our condition by calling it "the persecution of the righteous" (see Matthew 5:10). Or, we can choose to deny our declining condition altogether and rededicate ourselves even more to continuing our failing methods and structures, deluding ourselves into thinking that *this time* they will reward us with different results.

Or . . . *we can repent.*

We can choose to come face-to-face with reality. And what is reality? George Barna states it succinctly: "The stumbling block for the church is not its theology, but its failure to apply what it believes in a compelling way. . . . Christians have been their own worst enemies when it comes to showing the world what authentic, biblical Christianity looks like."[12]

Reality demands that we accept the perspective that the standards of our lifestyles are clearly too low, our design and structures too isolated and self-serving, our mission lopsidedly proclamational, our approach too self-righteous, and our name close to "mud." Then we can turn back to bridge building. Back to a humble and better "both/and" balance. Back to the pursuit of being Jesus' church of irresistible influence. And what will that require?

1. i² Will Require Pastors to Redefine Success.

Pastors are, and will continue to be, the key to the church. As shepherds, they are the primary shapers of church values, strategy, and direction. As they go, so go the people. They also define for their people what "success" is. But, unfortunately for many pastors, "success" revolves around growth, size, and numbers. The bigger the better. But is it?

When "success" becomes "size" in the heart of a pastor, compromises inevitably occur. This Baal inspires a false pride or a crushing sense of failure. Strategies become more and more about how to draw and keep people, how to make them happy and comfortable, and less and less "according to the will of God" (1 Peter 5:2 NASB). Sin can be, and often is, overlooked because dealing with it rocks the boat.

For the evangelical church to recapture its New Testament design, pastors must redefine success in their hearts and with each other as influence.

Although the Bible doesn't ignore the issue of size, it never reveres it. The tenor of Scripture is never "how many," but "how well." It's always quality over quantity. As a spiritual shepherd himself, Jesus often pruned his ranks (John 6) in order to insure a purer stock. In time, he knew, it would guarantee growth—but only as a result, never as the goal.

For the evangelical church to recapture its New Testament design, pastors must redefine success in their hearts and with each other as *influence*. How good are we? How much good are we doing for others? Are we an irresistible influence? Do we get results? Are our lives salty, is our witness light? For churches of the twenty-first century, that would be a profound, much-needed, and healthy adjustment leading to:

- Better lifestyles
- Strong, more compelling witness

- Authentic people
- Community bridges

But all this begins in the heart of a pastor. As the spiritual leader, the pastor sets both the tone and the path for what success is. And where he leads, people will follow.

2. i² Will Require the Church to Redesign Its Structure.

Most church structures (whether Sunday school, small groups, or what have you) are actually "holding tanks," relentlessly trying to help people while keeping them from falling away. While that is admirable in one sense, this structure in time actually inhibits personal growth rather than lifting it to higher levels. Eventually, people stagnate spiritually in these settings.

For the church to move itself back from the margins of American life and into a place of renewed influence, church design and structure must be radically overhauled to equip, support, and send people into satisfying and strategic areas of service. What we need in the twenty-first century are church structures that are redesigned to serve as "launching pads" rather than "holding tanks." Only then will the church unleash its people to reach for a greater maturity while offering compelling proof to the world that the truth it proclaims is worth considering.

Structure is the means to that kind of influence, not better preaching or grander events. Therefore, any church that is serious about developing its people and building bridges to its community will soon discover the "must" priority of redesigning its structure.

Of course, if you are like some who feel "stuck" when it comes to discussions of structure and organization, perhaps you or your leadership team could employ a church consultant. We have used consultants at Fellowship Bible Church for years, and they have proved enormously beneficial in helping us rightly align our structure with our desire to be influential.

3. i² Will Require Laypeople to Reconnect with a Lifestyle of Specific Spiritual Standards and Service.

What are the lifestyle distinctives of the evangelical? Increasingly, this is a hard question to answer, especially when, according to Barna, seven out of ten Christians are "prone to hedonistic attitudes about life."[13] The reality is that most Christians like to keep their lives spiritually undefined. This encourages a flabby, day-to-day morality that believes that as long as it doesn't hurt anyone, it's okay.

But such a lifestyle *does* hurt others; it seriously undermines public confidence in the church and its message. An onlooking public is tempted, with some justification, to express the objections of nineteenth-century philosopher Friedrich Nietzsche, who said that "in Christianity, neither morality nor religion come into contact with reality at any point." Without proof to the contrary presented in godly lifestyles, how do we refute such an accusation? The fact is, "to the average non-believer, Christians act no different than anyone else."[14]

Of course, the drawback here to spiritual influence should be painfully obvious. In an age when people are spiritually open but desperately hungering for proof, evangelical lifestyles are doing a better job of erecting roadblocks of cynicism than building bridges of influence.

That must change!

Churches must help their people define the Christian life with specifics, and laypeople, in turn, must become serious about embracing those standards. Otherwise, as Barna writes, "the greatest danger to the future of the evangelical church" will not be from without, but from ourselves, "in the quality of our witness."[15]

And then there is the issue of service, of "making your life count" for the kingdom. There, too, standards must be raised. The goal of the Christian life must be expanded beyond self-interests to the greater concerns of the world, not just for the sake of duty, but for the sake of life—the abundant life (John 10:10). The boredom and restlessness seen everywhere in the church, I believe, is due primarily to the smallness of our purpose. It's rarely bigger than the scope of our own personal needs.

The goal of the Christian life must be expanded beyond self-interests to the greater concerns of the world.

If Fellowship Bible Church has proven anything, it is how passionate people can become when they discover a calling higher than themselves—a calling that falls in line with the gifts and abilities God has given them. Those are electric connections that lead laypeople to a lifetime of spiritual adventure that goes far beyond the "holding tank" experiences most Christian people find themselves in now.

That is what i² means for the layperson. It requires a reconnection both to a lifestyle of spiritual specifics and to a service that inspires a lifetime of spiritual passion.

So this is where we must begin: with pastors personally embracing the higher goal of influence, with churches redesigning their structures, with laypeople rediscovering the real Christian life. If we labor faithfully, refusing to compromise or go back, our churches will slowly but surely transform themselves from fading lights back into guiding lights. And in the process, a bridge will appear—a bridge once again linking God's both/and purposes for the church with the real needs of the world.

A bridge of irresistible influence.

BRIDGE BUILDER QUESTIONS

Do you view evangelicalism as socially disconnected?

What practical steps could you take this next year to improve your church's name in the community?

Which of the three suggestions for calling the evangelical church to irresistible influence is most applicable to your church? What about to you personally?

NOTES

CHAPTER ONE

1. Elmer Towns and Warren Bird, *Into the Future: Turning Today's Church Trends into Tomorrow's Opportunities* (Grand Rapids: Revell, 2000), 37.

2. George Barna, *The Frog in the Kettle* (Ventura, Calif.: Regal, 1990), 138.

3. Ibid., 139.

4. David Wells, *Losing Our Virtue* (Grand Rapids: Eerdmans, 1998), 32.

5. Rick Warren, *The Purpose-Driven Church* (Grand Rapids: Zondervan, 1995), 56.

6. George Barna, *The Second Coming of the Church* (Nashville: Word, 1998), 6.

7. Dr. Henry Blackaby, quoted in a speech at the Billy Graham Training Center, May 22, 1999 (Leesburg, Va.: Intercessors for America).

8. Charles Chaney, *Church Planting at the End of the Twentieth Century* (Wheaton: Tyndale House, 1998), 60.

9. Michael Regele, "Death of the Church," *Mars Hill* (Summer 1998), 66.

10. David McCullough, *The Great Bridge: The Epic Story of the Building of the Brooklyn Bridge* (New York: Simon & Schuster, 1972), 77.

11. Bill Hull, *Can We Save the Evangelical Church?* (Old Tappan, N.J.: Revell, 1993), 7.

12. McCullough, *Great Bridge*, 80.

13. Ibid., 73.

14. Ibid., 82.

CHAPTER TWO

1. David McCullough, *The Great Bridge: The Epic Story of the Building of the Brooklyn Bridge* (New York: Simon & Schuster, 1972), 181.

2. Ibid.

3. Ibid., 183.

4. Henry Petroski, *Engineers of Dreams: Great Bridge Builders and the Spanning of America* (New York: Vintage, 1996), 54.

5. Elmer Towns, Warren Bird, and Leith Anderson, *Into the Future: Turning Today's Church Trends into Tomorrow's Opportunities* (Grand Rapids: Revell, 2000), 37.

6. George Weigel, quoted in Samuel P. Huntington, *The Clash of Civilizations and the Remaking of the World Order* (New York: Simon & Schuster, 1996), 96.

7. David Wells, *Losing Our Virtue* (Grand Rapids: Eerdmans, 1998), 17.

8. George Barna, *The Second Coming of the Church* (Nashville: Word, 1998), 5.

9. Rodney Stark, as quoted in Shaunti Feldhahn, *Y2K: The Millennium Bug* (Portland: Multnomah Press, 1998), 14.

10. Michael Green, *Evangelism in the Early Church* (London: Highland Books, 1970), 222–23; italics mine.

11. Feldhahn, *Y2K: The Millennium Bug*, 115.

12. Rodney Stark, "Live Longer, Healthier, and Better," *Christian History* (online), no. 57, www2.Christianity.net; italics mine.

13. Will Durant, *The Age of Faith* (New York: Simon & Schuster, 1950), 77–78; italics mine.

14. Tertullian, quoted in Will Durant, *Caesar and Christ* (New York: Simon & Schuster, 1944), 603.

15. Petroski, *Engineers of Dreams,* 56.

16. Ibid., 57.

17. Ibid.

CHAPTER THREE

1. Tom Horton and Barry Wolman, *Superspan: The Golden Gate Bridge* (San Francisco: Squarebooks, 1998), 23.

2. Michael Regele, "Death of the Church," *Mars Hill* (Summer 1998), 67.

3. Martin Lloyd-Jones, *Sermon on the Mount* (Grand Rapids: Eerdmans, 1959), 172.

CHAPTER FOUR

1. Quoted in David McCullough, *The Great Bridge: The Epic Story of the Building of the Brooklyn Bridge* (New York: Simon & Schuster, 1972), 80.

2. Judith Dupre, *Bridges* (New York: Black Dog & Leventhal, 1997), 44.

3. Michael Regele, "Death of the Church," *Mars Hill* (Summer 1998), 69.

4. George Barna, *The Frog in the Kettle* (Ventura, Calif.: Regal, 1990), 123.

5. Peter Drucker, *The Effective Executive* (New York: Harper & Row, 1966), 1–2.

CHAPTER FIVE

1. Walt Whitman, "Passage to India." As quoted in *Bartlett's Familiar Quotations* (Boston: Little, Brown, and Co., 1980), 576.

2. Joseph Rickaby.

CHAPTER SIX

1. Henry Petroski, *Engineers of Dreams: Great Bridge Builders and the Spanning of America* (New York: Vintage, 1996), 217.

CHAPTER NINE

1. Jack Dennison, *City Reaching: On the Road to Transformation* (Pasadena, Calif.: William Carey Library, 1999), 7.

2. Ibid., 49.

3. Ibid., 71.

CHAPTER TEN

1. David McCullough, *The Great Bridge: The Epic Story of the Building of the Brooklyn Bridge* (New York: Simon & Schuster, 1972), 154.

2. Ibid.

3. Rick Warren, *The Purpose-Driven Church* (Grand Rapids: Zondervan, 1995), 32.

4. George Barna, *The Second Coming of the Church* (Nashville: Word, 1998), 36.

5. Ibid., 101.

6. Ibid., 36.

7. Warren, *Purpose-Driven Church*, 384.

8. Bill Hull, *Can We Save the Evangelical Church?* (Old Tappan, N.J.: Revell, 1993), 56.

9. H. B. London, Pastor's Prayer Breakfast Address, North Little Rock, October 1999.

10. Barna, *Second Coming of the Church*, 173.

CHAPER ELEVEN

1. Judith Dupre, *Bridges* (New York: Black Dog & Leventhal, 1997), 105.

2. Daisy Bates, *The Long Shadow of Little Rock: A Memoir* (Little Rock: University of Arkansas Press, 1987), 72–76.

3. Jack Dennison, *City Reaching: On the Road to Transformation* (Pasadena, Calif.: William Carey Library, 1999), 173.

4. Michael Regele, "Death of the Church," *Mars Hill* (Summer 1998), 71.

5. Dennison, *City Reaching*, 155.

CHAPTER TWELVE

1. Drew Fetherston, *The Chunnel: The Amazing Story of the Undersea Crossing of the English Channel* (New York: Times Books, 1997), 247.

2. Ibid., 235.

3. Ibid., 237.

4. Ibid., 247.

5. John Stott, *Human Rights and Human Wrongs: Major Issues for a New Century* (Grand Rapids: Baker, 1999), 21.

6. Ray Stedman, Message 12 (Discovery Publishing, Catalogue 67, May 24, 1964), 1.

7. Stott, *Human Rights and Human Wrongs,* 21–25.

8. Jack Dennison, *City Reaching: On the Road to Transformation* (William Carey Library, 1999), 43.

9. Stott, *Human Rights and Human Wrongs,* 17.

10. George Barna, *The Frog in the Kettle* (Ventura, Calif.: Regal, 1990), 129.

11. Dennison, *City Reaching,* 41–42.

12. George Barna, *The Second Coming of the Church* (Nashville: Word, 1998), 5.

13. Barna, *Frog in the Kettle,* 9.

14. Ibid., 227.

15. Ibid., 122.

We want to hear from you. Please send your comments about this book to us in care of the address below. Thank you.

GRAND RAPIDS, MICHIGAN 49530 USA
WWW.ZONDERVAN.COM